The Illusions of Postmodernism

The Illusions of Postmodernism

Terry Eagleton

First published 1996
Reprinted 1997 (twice)

Blackwell Publishers Ltd
108 Cowley Road
Oxford OX4 1JF, UK

Blackwell Publishers Inc
350 Main Street
Malden, Massachusetts 02148, USA

British Library Cataloguing in Publication Data

A CIP catalogue record for this book is available from the British Library

Library of Congress Cataloging in Publication Data

Eagleton, Terry, 1943–
The illusions of postmodernism / Terry Eagleton
p. cm.
Includes bibliographical references (p.) and index.
ISBN 0–631–20322–2 (alk. paper)
ISBN 0–631–20323–0 (pbk : alk. paper)
1. Postmodernism. I. Title.
B831.2.E18 1996 96–8101
149—dc20 CIP

Typeset in 11.5 on 13.5pt Bembo
by Wearset, Boldon, Tyne and Wear
Printed and bound in Great Britain
by T. J. International Limited, Padstow, Cornwall

This book is printed on acid-free paper

Contents

region within contemporary life – is a matter of argument.

This distinction between postmodernism and postmodernity seems to me useful, but it is not one which I have particularly respected in this book. I have tended to stick to the more familiar term 'postmodernism' to cover both of these things, since they are clearly closely related. But my interest here is more in the ideas than in the artistic culture, which is why there is no discussion of particular works of art. There is not much discussion of particular theorists either, which may strike some as strange. But my concern is less with the more *recherché* formulations of postmodern philosophy than with the culture or milieu or even sensibility of postmodernism as a whole. I have in mind less the higher philosophical flights of the subject than what a particular kind of student today is likely to believe; and though I consider quite a lot of what they believe to be false, I have tried to say so in a way which might persuade them that they never believed it in the first place. In the process, I accuse postmodernism from time to time of 'straw-targeting' or caricaturing its opponents' positions, a charge which might well be turned back upon my own account. But this is partly because I have in my sights precisely such 'popular' brands of postmodern thought, and partly because postmodernism is such a portmanteau phenomenon that anything you assert of one piece of it is almost bound to be untrue of another. Thus some of the views I attribute to postmodernism in general might well be qualified or even rejected in the work of a particular theorist; but they constitute even so a kind of received wisdom, and to this extent I do not consider myself guilty of excessive travesty. On the contrary, though my review of the topic is generally a negative one, I have tried to give postmodernism its due where I can, drawing attention to its strengths along with its failings. It is not just a question of being pro- or anti-postmodern, though in my view it is more a question of being against rather than for. Just as 'postmodernist' itself means not just that you have left modernism definitively behind, but that you have worked your way through it to a position still deeply marked by it, so there may be a kind of pre-postmodernism which has worked its way through postmodernism and come out roughly on the side where it started, which is by no means the same as not having shifted at all.

Part of postmodernism's power is the fact it exists, whereas how true this is of socialism these days is rather more debatable. *Pace* Hegel, it would seem at present that what is real is irrational, and what is rational is unreal. Throughout this study, I have judged postmodernism from a broadly socialist perspective; but this should not of course be taken to imply that socialism does not have its problems too. On the contrary, it is now probably more plagued and notional an idea than at any stage in its turbulent career. It would be intellectual dishonesty to pretend that Marxism is any longer a living political reality, or that the prospects for socialist change, for the moment at least, are anything but exceedingly remote. It is just that it would be a good deal worse than dishonest in such circumstances to relinquish the vision of a just society, and so to acquiesce in the appalling mess which is the contemporary world. I am not, then, proposing that we have some fully-fledged alternative to postmodernism at our fingertips, just that we can do rather better; and one doesn't need to be a convinced socialist, let alone a devout Marxist, to concur with that.

A word, finally, on giving comfort to one's opponents. I have tried to criticize postmodernism from a political and theoretical perspective, rather than in the style of some banal common-sense reaction. But it is probably unavoidable that some of what I argue will be endorsed by conservatives who assail postmodernism for what I would myself consider all the most disreputable reasons. Radicals and conservatives, after all, necessarily share some ground in common, and if they did not would be incommensurable rather than at odds with one another. Radicals, for example, are traditionalists, just as conservatives are; it is simply that they adhere to entirely different traditions. Those postmodernists who hold that radicals should not criticize each other lest it delight the heart of reactionaries should recall the limits of a politics based on opportunism rather than truth, however much they would prefer the latter term to go in scare quotes. If conservative readers do indeed find themselves heartily endorsing the socialist transformation of society after reading the book, then I shall be delighted.

The most postmodernist aspect of this book is its shameless self-plagiarism. Though most of the text is original, I have stolen from some previous writings of my own, which appeared in the *London Review of Books*, *The Times Literary Supplement*, *The Monthly Review*, *Textual Practice* and *The Socialist Register*. I must thank the editors of these journals for their kind permission to reprint, and hope that no reader subscribes to them all. I am also deeply grateful to Peter Dews and Peter Osborne, who were generous enough to read this book in manuscript and make some strikingly helpful suggestions.

T. E.

1
Beginnings

Imagine a radical movement which had suffered an emphatic defeat. So emphatic, in fact, that it seemed unlikely to resurface for the length of a lifetime, if even then. The defeat I have in mind is not just the kind of rebuff with which the political left is depressingly familiar, but a repulse so definitive that it seemed to discredit the very paradigms with which such politics had traditionally worked. It would now be less a matter of hotly contesting these notions than of contemplating them with something of the mild antiquarian interest with which one might regard Ptolemaic cosmology or the scholasticism of Duns Scotus. They, and the language of conventional society, would now seem less ferociously at odds than simply incommensurable – the discourses of different planets rather than of adjacent nations. What if the left were suddenly to find itself less overwhelmed or out-manoeuvred than simply washed up, speaking a discourse so quaintly out of tune with the modern era that, as with the language of Gnosticism or courtly love, nobody even bothered any longer to enquire into its truth value? What if the vanguard were to become the remnant, its arguments still dimly intelligible but spinning off rapidly into some metaphysical outer space where they became nothing but a muffled cry?

What would be the likely reaction of the political left to such a defeat?

Many, no doubt, would drift either cynically or sincerely to the right, regretting their earlier views as infantile idealism. Others would keep the faith out of habit or nostalgia, clinging anxiously to an imaginary identity and risking the neurosis which this is likely to bring in its wake. There are, after all, those devotees for whom nothing whatsoever could count as a falsification of their beliefs – those Christians, for example, who true to what the philosophers of science call the 'underdetermination of data by theory', would continue to gather joyfully around the eucharistic table even if it had been shown to everyone else's satisfaction that the gospels were fraudulent from start to finish. Indeed there are members of the Anglican church today who behave in more or less this way. But other responses could be expected too. A small clutch of left triumphalists, incurably sanguine, would no doubt carry on detecting impending signs of revolution in the faintest flicker of militancy. In others the radical impulse would persist, but would be forced to migrate elsewhere. The governing assumption of such an epoch, one imagines, would be that the system itself was unbreachable; and a great many radical positions which might seem superficially unrelated could be seen to flow from this gloomy presupposition.

One might expect, for example, that there would be an upsurge of interest in the margins and crevices of the system – in those ambiguous, indeterminate spots where its power seemed less implacable, the shadowy margins where it trailed off into silence. The system could not be breached; but it could at least be momentarily transgressed, probed for those neuralgic points where its authority faltered and unravelled. Fascinated by these fault-lines, one might even come to imagine that there *is* no centre to society after all; but while this might be a convenient way of rationalizing one's own lack of power, it could only be at the cost of acknowledging that there can logically be no margins either. One might expect this fact itself might be calculated into the theory – that a bleak awareness of the collusion between centre and margins, power and rupture, of the stealthy cat-and-mouse game played out between them, would go hand in hand with a more heady affirmation of whatever the system itself expelled as so much detritus, of whatever its ruling rationality seemed not to incorporate. One could envisage much celebration of the marginal and minority as positive in themselves – an absurd enough view, of course, since margins and minorities currently include neo-Nazis, UFO buffs, the international bourgeoisie and those who believe in lashing delinquent adolescents until the blood runs down their thighs. The idea of a creative *majority* movement, for this habit of mind as much as for the old-style liberalism of a John Stuart Mill, would come to seem like a contradiction in terms, precisely because this style of thought, suitably amnesiac, could no longer remember any instance of a beneficent system or an appealing mass movement. At its extreme, such a case ought to find it hard to cope with a previously marginal current becoming politically dominant (the African National Congress, for example), given its formalist prejudice against 'dominance' as such. Logically speaking, it could only hope that its own values would never come to power. The ideas of system, consensus and organization would themselves become demonized in vaguely anarchistic fashion, denounced as absolute ills by those committed to a tolerant relativism.

The historical basis of this belief would be that political movements which were at once mass, central and productive had temporarily gone out of business; but it ill befits an historicizing brand of thought to generalize this to a universal doctrine. It would be the theory of those who were too young to recall a mass radical politics, but who had a good deal of glum experience of drearily oppressive majorities. The notions of law and authority might also be indiscriminately devalued, as though there was no such thing as a protective law or a benign authority. Theorists would mock the madness of the Law in suburban enclaves protected by private security guards, celebrating transgression as inherently good while worrying about child abuse. Protest would still be possible; but because the system would instantly recongeal around this irritant like a jellyfish, the radical sensibility would be accordingly divided – between a brittle pessimism on the one hand, and an exhilarated vision of ceaseless difference, mobility, disruption on the other. The distance between all that, and the drearily determinate world of social and economic life, would no doubt bulk embarrassingly large; but the gap might be narrowed if one were to attend to those few surviving enclaves where these things could still find a home, where a pleasure and playfulness not wholly under the heel of power might still be relished. Primary candidates for this role might be language and sexuality, and one would accordingly anticipate an enormous inflation of interest in these matters in the period in question. Conference papers entitled 'Putting the anus back into *Coriolanus*' would attract hordes of excited acolytes who knew little about the bourgeoisie but a good deal about buggery. The split between pessimism and euphoria, however, might resurface here too: some thinkers would caution how discourse and sexuality were themselves policed, regulated, heavy with power, while others would continue to dream of a liberated signifier or an unshackled sexuality. The radical impulse would not be abandoned; but it would shift gradually from the transformative to the subversive, and nobody except the advertisers would speak of revolution any more. The elation of an earlier, more hopeful phase of radicalism would survive, but it would now be blended with the hard-boiled pragmatism of its disillusioned aftermath, to give birth to a fresh style of left ideology which one might dub libertarian pessimism. One would continue to dream of a utopian other to the system, indeed to the whole concept of system or regime as such, while grimly insisting on the recalcitrance of power, the frailty of the ego, the absorptive power of capital, the insatiability of desire, the inescapability of the metaphysical, the ineluctability of the Law, the indeterminable effects of political action, and so of the sheer gullibility of one's own most secret hopes. The dream of liberation would not be relinquished, however much one would scorn the naivety of those foolish enough to believe it could ever be realized. It would not be out of the question to run across people who wished to see the Epoch of Man pass away, and voted Liberal Democrat.

There are other reasons why one might expect a cult of ambiguity and indeterminacy in these conditions. In certain robustly entrepreneurial nations, where the word 'aggressive' is used as a compliment and feeling negative about something is regarded as a moral failing, ideas of hesitancy, negativity, undecidability and the like might well loom up as the most radical thing since the Long March. But it is also true that rigorous, determinate knowledge is rather less in demand when there seems no question of a full-blooded political transformation. There is no point in labouring away in the British Museum, absorbing great swathes of indigestible economic theory, if the system is simply impregnable. One of the most moving narratives of modern history is the story of how men and women languishing under various forms of oppression came to acquire, often at great personal cost, the sort of technical knowledge necessary for them to understand their own condition more deeply, and so to acquire some of the theoretical armoury essential to change it. It is an insult to inform these men and women that, in the economic metaphor for intellectual life now prevalent in the USA, they are simply 'buying into' the conceptual closures of their masters, or colluding with phallocentrism. Those who are privileged enough not to need to know, for whom there is nothing politically at stake in reasonably accurate cognition, have little to lose by proclaiming the virtues of undecidability. There is no reason why literary critics should not turn to autobiography or anecdotalism, or simply slice up their texts and deliver them to their publishers in a cardboard box, if they are not so politically placed as to need emancipatory knowledge.

If the system is deemed all-powerful, a view which overlooks the fact that it is at once formidably resourceful and spectacularly unsuccessful, then the sources of opposition can only be found outside it. But if it is really all-powerful then there can by definition be nothing outside it, any more than there could be anything outside the infinite curvature of cosmic space. If the system is everywhere, then like the Almighty herself it puts in an appearance at no point in particular, and so is invisible, and thus can be said to be no sort of system at all. The pan-systemic, given a mild shove, can mutate into the anti-systemic. There is a thin line between claiming that totality is sublimely unrepresentable, and asserting that it doesn't exist. What this latter claim might mean, presumably, is that a certain classical, 'centred' sort of system no longer exists; but those avant-gardists who insisted on defining *system as such* in this quaintly old-fashioned way might naturally be led to conclude that it had evaporated altogether. Even if it existed, and even if there *were* something outside it, then whatever that was would be less oppositional than incommensurable, unable to gain any effective leverage on the system itself. If such a force were drawn into the orbit of the system so as to challenge it, its otherness would be instantly contaminated and its subversive power would dwindle to nothing. Whatever negates the system in theory is thus logically incapable of doing so in practice. There might well be some alterity to everything we have, indeed it might be brushing our skin and drifting under our fingertips at this very moment; but we are powerless to name it, since to do so is already to have erased it. Anything we could understand would be by that token complicit with our degraded logics, and so incapable of saving us, while the genuinely outlandish or subversive would fall clean outside our frames of representation and be struck as idle as Kant's mysterious *noumenon*.

One would expect, then, that such a political period would be rife with various veins of pseudo-mysticism, enamoured of whatever gives the slip to the concept, enthralled by those spasms of the mind which confound its customary distinctions, which breed in us some ecstatic state of indeterminacy in which the border between identity and non-identity is transcended (though we could not of course *know* this), and the logical deadlock I have just described is dissolved rather than resolved. Such 'thought' would at once be preciously utopian, running up its head against the limits of language in order to glimpse some currently inconceivable state beyond it, and a fantastic displacement of a genuine political deadlock. In an interesting ambivalence, one might expect to find some radicals denouncing a totality they took to be real, and others dismissing the whole affair as a figment of the overheated, compulsively totalizing brain. Some, one might predict, would assume that the dominant system was entirely negative – that nothing *within* this seamlessly non-contradictory whole could by definition be of value – and turn from it in dismay to idealize some numinous Other. This cult would no doubt be coupled with a guilty self-laceration on the part of some scions of the first world who would hanker to be just about anybody but themselves. One might forecast an enormous upsurge of interest in the alien, deviant, exotic, unincorporable. Perhaps there would be a quickening of concern for non-human animals; or perhaps radical theorists would be frantically trying to communicate with aardvarks or the inhabitants of Alpha Centauri, while hoping of course that their communications would remain suitably unintelligible.

Other thinkers, less romantically ultra-leftist, would no doubt strive to invent a new version of the classical notion of 'immanent critique', convinced that there was that within the logic of the system which, prised open or practised upon in a certain way, could be used to undermine it. For the traditional idea of immanent critique, it is at those points where a system is structurally non-identical with itself that it is hollowed out by the shadow of an alternative political future, so that the distinction between 'inside' and 'outside' is in this sense deconstructed. Just as there are ways of following rules which end up by transforming them, or where the rules intimate to you when to throw them away, so there is that within any system which inscribes its otherness within its interiority. One might redescribe this old-fashioned idea of immanent critique as, say, a 'deconstruction'. But this, in its newly fashionable forms, could only ever be a strategic skirmish or fleeting subversion, a rapid guerrilla raid on the fortress of Reason, since for it to become systemic would be for it to fall victim to the very logic it threw into question. It would be a critique conducted more at the level of the mind than at the level of political forces; indeed one might understand it, in part, as exactly such a displacement. It would be a Dadaist form of politics, wedded to the dissident gesture, the iconoclastic refusal, the inexplicable happening. If a weighty theorist of carnival were to be unearthed at this point, one who celebrated a sporadic disruption which could in no way dismantle the Law it parodied, one might confidently anticipate that he or she would swiftly give birth to a major scholarly industry. Grotesquerie would be all the rage, while monsters and masochism would surge in the intellectual stockmarket.

Behind this brand of thought would lurk the assumption that the idea of a *creative system* was an oxymoron, and the notion of a creative anti-system a tautology. And behind this, in turn, would lie the historical fact that that there were precious few instances of a creative political system on offer. Were this not so, then one could easily imagine the whole of this style of thought being transfigured at a stroke. If its exponents had belonged to a different historical era – had been in, say, on the tumultuous birth of a new, inspiring form of social life – then it is morally certain that they would not hold many of the doctrines they did. While a mass radical movement is still on the boil, it is not hard to overturn a simplistic binary opposition between the System and its Others, the former demonized and the latter angelized, since those 'others' are clearly products of the system itself, and know themselves to be such. It is exactly because they play some reasonably central role in it that they have the power to change it. But it is also easier to dismiss the idea that such immanent critique can only ever be spasmodic, tactical, or a minority affair. For what would be clear is that there are *contradictory systems*, whole alternative life-forms at loggerheads with one another; and that any formalistic distinction between 'system' on the one hand, and 'dissent' on the other, is simply implausible. Those who rummage around for some convenient force to put against 'the system' are usually full-blooded monists decked out in pluralist clothing, forgetful that 'the system' itself is conflictive and contradictory to its core. That it is hard to feel this in the tranquillity of Oxford or Santa Cruz is no decent excuse for the oversight.

For radicals to discard the idea of totality in a rush of holophobia is, among other more positive things, to furnish themselves with some much-needed consolation. For in a period when no very far-reaching political action seems really feasible, when so-called micropolitics seems the order of the day, it is relieving to convert this necessity into a virtue – to persuade oneself that one's political limits have, as it were, a solid ontological grounding, in the fact that social totality is in any case a chimera. It doesn't matter if there is no political agent on hand to transform the whole, since there is in fact no whole to be transformed. It is as though, having mislaid the breadknife, one declares the loaf to be already sliced. Totalities, after all, have to exist for someone; and there would now seem nobody for whom the totality was a totality for. It has traditionally been thought to be for groups who urgently need to make some overall sense of their oppressive conditions in order to set about changing them. Just to be free and happy, some people need to grasp the way their specific situation interlocks with a larger context, whose logic helps to determine their destiny. All totalities are launched from highly particular situations, and this is one of several ways we shall be considering in which universality, and difference or specificity, are by no means simple opposites.

If these interlockings do not show up spontaneously in common experience, then one can, as a good empiricist, seize on this fact to cast doubt on the whole notion of an overall system. Alternatively, one can ask whether there might not be mechanisms which accounted for this hiatus between how things are and how they seem. Nobody of course has ever actually *seen* a system, any more than anyone has clapped eyes on the Freudian id, the University of Cambridge or the Save the Children Fund; but it seems rash to conclude from this that none of them actually exists. It is rather a matter of speculating whether there might not be certain regular effects in our daily life which we can make plausible sense of by positing the impact upon it of a coherent, if invisible, set of forces. This, after all, was how Freud came to disinter the unconscious, an entity devoutly defended by some of those who doubt we can speak coherently of the transnational capitalist system. Such a speculation makes no claims as it stands about the *nature* of this system – whether it is centred or centreless, unified or asymmetrical, informed by a determining principle or reducible to a singular essence. But one can always of course make life easy for oneself by identifying the whole notion of system with some simple-minded essentialism, thus allowing the concept to obediently write itself off.

The point, anyway, is that the concept of totality implies a subject for whom it would make some practical difference; but once such a subject has been rolled back, incorporated, scattered or metamorphosed out of existence, then the concept of totality is likely to fall with it. Unless, that is, one wants to preserve the idea of subversion in the absence of any likely agent of it, in which case you can always claim that the system subverts itself, and so combine a certain scepticism with a certain radicalism. But in general there would now seem nobody for whom the idea had much of a function, as it would, say, in an era of revolutionary nationalism; and like Bishop Berkeley's tree it would therefore lapse discreetly from existence just because no one was looking at it. The theoretical discrediting of the idea of totality, then, is to be expected in an epoch of political defeat for the left. Much of the scepticism of it, after all, hails from intellectuals who have no particularly pressing reason to locate their own social existence within a broader political framework. There are others, however, who are not quite so fortunate. It is not, then, just a choice between alternative ways of seeing, as though there are those megalomaniac, phallus-struck theorists who like their ideas to come big and full-blooded, and those more modest, particularizing thinkers who prefer to stick with a politics so tiny as to be well-nigh invisible. To think of this as a choice of intellectual styles is itself an idealist move. How 'global' your thinking is depends not on how impressively thick you want your books to be, but on where you happen to be standing, not least if you would prefer to be standing somewhere else.

There are those radical thinkers who genuinely believe that a belief in totality is just a mesmerizing hindrance to real political change, as with the kind of mentally blocked student who feels unable to say anything unless he or she has grasped everything. Anti-totality may here be more of a strategic than a theoretical point: there may well be some sort of total system, but since our political actions cannot dent it as a whole we would be better advised to trim our sails and stick to more modest but more viable projects. This is a case to be respected, if not necessarily endorsed. Others object to the notion of society as a whole for much the same reason that Margaret Thatcher did. Not looking for totality is just code for not looking at capitalism. But a scepticism of totalities, left or right, is usually fairly bogus. It generally turns out to mean a suspicion of certain kinds of totality and an enthusiastic endorsement of others. Some kinds of totality – prisons, patriarchy, the body, absolutist political orders – would be acceptable topics of conversation, while others – modes of production, social formations, doctrinal systems – would be silently censored. Perhaps it might be thought that all totalities are 'essentialist', reducible to some single determining principle; but this is not the case, for example, with the charming north Devonshire village of Porlock. Porlock, one might claim, is certainly a totality of a kind: one is almost never in doubt about where it begins and ends, or likely to confuse it with the next village along the coast. Its boundaries are firmly etched, and it is quite evidently itself and not some other thing. But it is questionable even so that Porlock can be reduced to some single animating force, such as the high street or the flower shop, which informs all of its constituent parts with impeccable even-handedness. There is no reason to assume that totalities are always homogeneous; and if the globe is indeed becoming a more dismally self-identical place, this has rather more to do with the operations of transnational capitalism, and the cultural forms it brings in its wake, than with the paranoia of left political theorists. The idea that totality is all in the mind is a remarkably idealist doctrine for a supposedly materialist creed.

Grasping the shape of a totality requires some tiresomely rigorous thought, which is one reason why those who don't need to do it can revel in ambiguity and indeterminacy. There are those who need to know roughly how things stand with them in order to be free, and those for whom phrases like 'how things stand' smack of objectivism, scientism, phallocentrism, transcendentally disinterested subjects and a number of other creepy affairs. (There would also seem to be those for whom utterances like 'Lord John Russell then became Prime Minister' are insidious instances of 'positivism'.) In the imaginary epoch we are postulating, we might expect that a good deal of blood and ink would be spilt over questions of epistemology – oddly, in a way, since this is hardly the most world-shaking area of philosophical inquiry. But there would presumably be a need to account for how and whether we can know the world in the face of the apparent collapse of some classical epistemological models, a collapse closely related to the loss of a sense of political agency. For practice is of course one of the primary ways in which we encounter the world; and if any very ambitious forms of it are denied us, then it is not long before we will catch ourselves wondering whether there is really anything out there, or at least anything quite so fascinating as ourselves. Perhaps we are all simply trapped within the prison house of our discourse. It is a revealing metaphor, which grasps language as obstacle rather than horizon, and one could imagine a bodily analogy to it: If only I could get out of my own head I could see whether there was anything out there. If only I could escape from behind the walls of my body I could encounter the world directly. As it is, I have to operate upon it in this lumbering, long-range fashion. But a body of course just is a way of acting upon the world, a mode of access to it, a point from which a world is coherently organized. 'A body is where there is something to be done', as Maurice Merleau-Ponty once put it. Just the same is true of language, the inside of which is also an outside, whose 'interior' is constituted as a ceaseless opening to an 'exterior', a constant self-surpassing or surge towards objects which dismantles the distinction between immanent and transcendent, since the one is inscribed within the other. (Why, Ludwig Wittgenstein once wondered, do we speak of the 'external' world? External to what?) To inhabit a language is already by that very token to inhabit a good deal more than it, and that there is that which transcends language is exactly what the interior of our language informs us of. Discourse can be obfuscating, to be sure – but not because it intervenes between me and the world, any more than I have to blunder from my arm to the coffee cup it grasps.

It would come as no surprise, then, to find the political left obsessed in such an era by epistemology, though it would take rather less than a cynic to suspect that some of this morbid fascination might well be a form of political displacement. Talk of whether the signifier produces the signified or vice versa, valuable though it doubtless is, is not quite what stormed the Winter Palace or brought down the Heath government. But there are, as usual, political conditions for such political displacement. When a radical movement is making headway, its epistemology is likely to be closely conditioned by its practice. It requires no esoteric theory at such times to recognize that the material world is at least real enough to be acted upon and altered; or that it is also, for rather too much of the time, dense and autonomous enough to resist one's designs upon it; or that one's theoretical doctrines or political desires may need to be reshaped to suit its imperious demands. It is also usually apparent that a cognitive error – say, mistaking the ruling class you confront for a gang of late-feudalist robber barons when they are actually a bunch of merchant bankers – will tend to breed embarrassing effects in one's political practice.

In such circumstances, you can always heed the advice of the pragmatists and see your cognitive propositions simply as ways of promoting your desired political goals; but if you do not wish to end up as a Stalinist you would be well counselled not to do so. Stalinist epistemology is precisely of such a kind. The point, anyway, is that questions of epistemology are deeply bound up with matters of political history. Once some ambitious political experiment has run aground, the realist assumptions implicit in such practice are bound to seem less persuasive. Some form of idealism might then well move in to replace them, though of a suitably new-fangled kind: in an epoch when talk of 'consciousness' had ceased to be sexy, it would be more advisable to speak of the world being constructed by, say, discourse rather than by the mind, even though it might come in some respects to much the same thing. Everything would become an interpretation, including that claim itself, in which case the idea of interpretation would cancel all the way through and leave everything exactly as it was. A radical epistemology would issue, conveniently enough, in a conservative politics. If discourse goes all the way down, it becomes as much a privileged *a priori* as the most rampant metaphysical idealism – that which, like God or *Geist*, we are unable to get behind any more than we can leap out of our skins. It would no doubt be crass sociological reductionism to see the difference between experiencing the world as material resistance, and regarding it as an effect of discourse, as a distinction between manual and mental labour, or between citizen and intellectual. It would also be imprudent to ignore such a refreshingly vulgar claim altogether. It would not be entirely surprising if the chief exponents of such theories turned out to be literary and philosophical types – if there were, for example, few practising historians, and certainly no practising scientists, among the most commonly touted names. This new idealism would no doubt go hand in hand with that particular form of reductionism known as culturalism, of which I shall have more to say later, which drastically undervalues what men and women have in common as natural, material creatures, foolishly suspects all talk of nature as insidiously mystifying, and overestimates the significance of cultural difference.

These are not, to be sure, the only reasons why epistemology is likely to be pitched into crisis in such a period. One would expect a host of such causes, a few of them to do with how social reality presents itself to us in the society of the spectacle. Nobody who emerges from a regular eight-hours-a-day television viewing is likely to be quite the same self-identical subject who once conquered India or annexed the Caribbean. The epistemology of the disco or shopping mall is hardly the epistemology of the jury, chapel or voting booth. In these circumstances, we might expect to find forms of subjectivity dramatically at odds with each other, as human subjects too stolidly self-identical to be open to otherness came eyeball-to-eyeball with human subjects too decentred to have much to open up in the first place. Subjects as producers and subjects as consumers, strenuous self-authors and laid-back self-eccentrics, would mingle incongruously in the same body. When Stuart Hall writes that 'We can no longer conceive of "the individual" in terms of a whole, centred, stable and completed Ego',[1] one feels tempted to inquire, in what is admittedly a hackneyed left gesture, just who this 'we' is meant to signify. Does it include bishops and bank managers? Is the unified subject merely a form of false consciousness, to be dispersed by a touch of deconstruction or an expansion of consumerism? And if so, why do its critics also oppose the notion of false consciousness?

Much of this would no doubt have felt different in an age of political militancy. In such a period, no one would need to resort to Godard or Mallarmé to know what being 'decentred' felt like; it is just that the decentring in question would be of an 'intentional' or 'transitive' kind, towards certain projects and into intricate solidarities with others, rather than some 'intransitive' condition or steady ontological state along the lines of a nasty bout of influenza. Human subjects who were seamlessly self-identical, who could name themselves with any assurance, would experience no need to revolt in the first place. Yet neither could such rebellion succeed unless its agents were also, however provisionally, self-affirmative and tolerably secure, equipped with determinate purposes and self-identical enough to carry them through. Such ambitious political actions, in other words, promise to deconstruct the tedious opposition between 'humanist' and 'anti-humanist', self-determining subjects and selves which are the effects of process, individuals of a bulging Bakhtinian repleteness and those of an alarming Lacanian leanness. When such enterprises are baffled, it is hardly surprising that these oppositions should rip open with such compulsively repetitive force. In the epoch we are imagining, what might gradually implode, along with a faith in the kind of reasonably certain knowledge we in fact enjoy all the time, would be the idea of a human subject unified enough to embark on significantly transformative action. Instead, one would hymn the praises of the schizoid, dishevelled subject, whose ability to fasten its own shoelaces, let alone topple the political state, would be bound to remain something of a mystery. And this, once more, would be among other things to make a theoretical virtue out of historical necessity. At the same time, it might provide us with some enormously fertile ways of thinking ourselves past the very self-identical, self-authoring subjects who had landed us in this political mess in the first place.

What else might one forecast of such an age? There would no doubt be a widespread loss of faith in the idea of teleology, given a chronically short supply of purposive historical action. Such a scepticism could by no means be reduced to this fact, but neither could it be wholly divorced from it. Given the assumption that a uniformly oppressive regime now regulated everything, it would also seem understandable to look around for some sector of life where a degree of pleasure, randomness or freedom might still precariously survive. Perhaps you might call this textuality, or language, or desire, or the body, or the unconscious. It would be ironic, incidentally, if the idea that desire is primary was thought to be a criticism of the Enlightenment, since from Hobbes to Holbach this is precisely an Enlightenment creed. One might predict a quickening interest in psychoanalysis, which among other finer things is the thinking person's pulp fiction, at once strenuously analytic and luridly sensational. If it had never existed, dissident intellectuals would surely have had to invent it. Psychoanalysis is also in some sense a radical discourse, but not in a way which has any very concrete or immediate political implications. It would thus figure as an appropriate kind of language for radical energies in a politically disorientated age.

If the more abstract questions of state, class, mode of production, economic justice, had proved for the moment too hard to crack, one might always shift one's attention to something more intimate and immediate, more sensuous and particular. One might expect the rise of a new somatics, in which the body was now the chief theoretical protagonist. Indeed there would no doubt soon be more bodies in literary criticism than on the fields of Waterloo. I shall be looking at this topic a little later; meanwhile it is worth speculating that language or textuality might also become such residual regions of freedom in a grimly quantified world, and one could imagine this leading in time to an incomparable enrichment of our understanding of them, in an arrestingly original new set of philosophical motifs. But it might also be possible to see how this acted at once as deepening and displacement. The terrors and allures of the signifier, its snares, seductions and subversions: all of this might figure at once as a bracingly novel form of politics, and as a glamorous substitute for baulked political energies, an ersatz iconoclasm in a politically quiescent society. It would be as though all the high drama, all the self-risking and extravagant expenditure which might have belonged to our moral and political life together in more propitious historical conditions, had now been thrust back into the contemplative theatre of reading, where these thwarted impulses could at least be kept warm, and where certain adventurous undoings which were no longer possible in political reality could be vicariously nurtured at the level of discourse. There would be a striking contrast between the bleak regimentation of social life on the one hand, and the spills and skids of the signifier on the other; and one might even imagine some theorists seeking to counter the accusation that it was all far removed from a humdrum reality by the pre-emptive strike of modelling the world itself on a book.

The cult of the text would thus fulfil the ambivalent function of all utopia: to provide us with a frail image of a freedom we might otherwise fail to commemorate, but in doing so to confiscate some of the energies which we might have invested in its actual realization. And one can imagine this exorbitation of discourse extending further than just the text, to encompass speech habits in general. If it is no longer possible to realize one's political desires in action, then one might direct them instead into the sign, cleansing it, for example, of its political impurities, and channelling into some linguistic campaign all the pent-up energies which can no longer help to end an imperialist war or bring down the White House. Language, of course, is as real as anything else, as those who are the objects or racial or sexist slurs have reason to know, and courteous or comradely speech is a necessary part of social life. But language, like anything else, can also come to figure as a fetish – both in the Marxist sense of being reified, invested with too numinous a power, and in the Freudian sense of standing in for something now elusively absent. To deny that there is any significant distinction between discourse and reality, between practising genocide and talking about it, is among other things a rationalization of this condition. Whether one projects language into material reality, or material reality into language, the result is to confirm that there is nothing as important as speaking. And if this itself does not speak eloquently of the deadlocked political situation of a highly specific corner of the globe, then it is hard to know what does. Those most sensitive to questions of correct ethnic terminology would then be indulging in a thoroughly ethnocentric practice.

There is one further speculation we might make about such a period, one so grossly improbable that I advance it with the greatest hesitancy. It is not out of the question that, in the apparent absence of any 'other' to the prevailing system, any utopic space beyond it, some of the more desperate theoreticians of the day might come to find the other of the system in itself. They might, in other words, come to project utopia onto what we actually have, finding in, say, the mobilities and transgressions of the capitalist order, the hedonism and pluralities of the marketplace, the circulation of intensities in media and disco, a freedom and fulfilment which the more puritanical politicos among us still grimly defer to some ever-receding future. They might fold the future into the present and thus bring history slithering abruptly to a halt. If this were to happen, it would be worth asking ourselves who has the authority to blow the whistle and call history off. What are the historical conditions of the promulgation of the end of history? Is this a performative masquerading as a constative, as you might announce that it had stopped raining because you were desperate to get out of the house? Has history, in the sense of modernity, come to end because we have triumphantly resolved its problems, or because they now strike us (who?) as pseudo-problems, or because we have finally given up on the task? If there never was any inner dynamic to history, wasn't it off already? Is all of it over, or just certain bits of it? The emancipation of oppressed peoples as well as the domination of Nature? And if foundations are now over, why is there so much foundationalism around? Why does the good news of the end of ideology appear to have seeped through to Berkeley or Bologna, but not to Utah or Ulster? One might expect this premature utopianism to be coupled with a celebration of popular culture as wholly positive, as undeniably democratic rather than as positive and manipulative together. Radicals, like anyone else, can come to hug their chains, decorate their prison cells, rearrange the deckchairs on the *Titanic* and discover true freedom in dire necessity. But this – the final identity between the system and its negation – is so cynical a suggestion that it is remarkably hard to picture.

Imagine, finally, the most bizarre possibility of all. I have spoken of symptoms of political defeat; *but what if this defeat never really happened in the first place?* What if it were less a matter of the left rising up and being forced back, than of a steady disintegration, a gradual failure of nerve, a creeping paralysis? What if the confrontation never quite took place, but people *behaved* as though it did? As though someone were to display all the symptoms of rabies, but had never been within biting distance of a mad dog.

2

Ambivalences

There is, of course, no need to *imagine* such a period at all. It is the one we are living in, and its name is postmodernism – though how far down this goes, whether it is wall-to-wall, is a matter of debate. Is anything to be gained, then, by the tiresome rhetorical ploy of pretending to forecast what is already staring us in the face? The point of taking a leaf out of postmodernism's book by fictionalizing it in this way, treating it as a possible rather than an actual world, is to estrange it to the point where we might be able to grasp something of its historical logic. It is as though, putting the actual phenomenon in brackets, we could have deduced much of it anyway from the bald fact of a perceived political defeat – as though we could work backwards from that datum and arrive by way of this thought experiment at the genuine article, reinventing its various aspects in purely theoretical spirit until they came to correspond magically with the real thing.

This, need one say, is in some sense an outrageous sleight of hand. Nobody could actually read off deconstruction or political correctness from the winding down of working-class militancy or the scuppering of the student movement. Historical necessity can only ever appear retrospectively, as a construct or hypothesis after the event. And there is of course nothing necessary in any case about postmodernism, as its own apologists for the aleatory would surely agree, since there are many possible aftermaths to a supposed political trouncing. But if forecasting the future with the benefit of the backward glance lends a spurious inevitability to what need never have come about in the first place, it does so for the sake of reminding us that not any old future will do – that postmodern culture, so we can now appreciate, was one particularly *plausible* future for that particular past, as the last Act of *King Lear* makes sense in terms of four preceding ones which never in the least dictated it. Wherever else postmodernism may spring from – 'post-industrial' society, the final discrediting of modernity, the recrudescence of the avant-garde, the commodification of culture, the emergence of vital new political forces, the collapse of certain classical ideologies of society and the subject – it is also, and centrally, the upshot of a political failure which it has either thrust into oblivion, or with which it has never ceased to shadow-box.

One would not expect postmodernists themselves to greet this proposition with acclaim. Nobody much likes being informed that they are the effect of an historical failure, any more than we take kindly to being told that we are the spawn of Satan. It is hardly, in either case, the most heroic of origins. Is not such a narrative merely another instance of the linear, historicist, reductionist teleology which postmodernism itself rejects out of hand? We will be looking at historicism a little later; but if the narrative need not be reductionist, it is because it would be absurd to imagine that this is *all* that postmodernism is. For one thing, quite a bit of it harks back to high modernism itself, whatever its own occasional protests to the contrary, which thus lends it a lengthier pedigree than any mere post-1960s phenomenon. For another thing, it is hard to see how Madonna or mock-Gothic buildings or the fiction of Martin Amis are the offspring of a political rout, though some enterprising cultural critic might no doubt try it on.

If postmodernism covers everything from punk rock to the death of metanarrative, fanzines to Foucault, then it is difficult to see how any single explanatory scheme could do justice to such a bizarrely heterogeneous entity. And if the creature is so diverse then it is hard to see how one could be in some simple sense either for or against it, any more than one could be for or against Peru. If there is any unity to postmodernism at all, then it can only be a matter of Wittgensteinian 'family resemblances'; and in this sense it seems to provide an instructive example of its own dogmatic anti-essentialism, of which more later on. If postmodernism were nothing but the backwash of a political débâcle, it would be hard, impressionistically speaking, to account for its often exuberant tone, and impossible to account for any of its more positive attributes. One would, for example, be forced to claim that its single most enduring achievement – the fact that it has helped to place questions of sexuality, gender and ethnicity so firmly on the political agenda that it is impossible to imagine them being erased without an almighty struggle – was nothing more than a substitute for more classical forms of radical politics, which dealt in class, state, ideology, revolution, material modes of production.[1]

That postmodernism's privileged political topics are indeed, among other things, substitutionary seems to me undeniable. Nobody who has run across the feeble concept of 'classism', which seems to come down to not feeling socially superior to people, or who has observed the lamentable effects on some postmodernist debates about gender or neo-colonialism of their ignorance of class structure and material conditions, could underestimate for a moment the disastrous political losses at stake here. The West is now bulging at the seams with political radicals whose ignorance of socialist traditions, not least their own, is certainly among other things the effect of postmodernist amnesia. And we are speaking here of the greatest reform movement that history has ever witnessed. We now find ourselves confronted with the mildly farcical situation of a cultural left which maintains an indifferent or embarrassed silence about that power which is the invisible colour of daily life itself, which determines our existence – sometimes literally so – in almost every quarter, which decides in large measure the destiny of nations and the internecine conflicts between them. It is as though almost every other form of oppressive system – state, media, patriarchy, racism, neo-colonialism –

can be readily debated, but not the one which so often sets the long-term agenda for all of these matters, or is at the very least implicated with them to their roots.

The power of capital is now so drearily familiar, so sublimely omnipotent and omnipresent, that even large sectors of the left have succeeded in naturalizing it, taking it for granted as such an unbudgable structure that it is as though they hardly have the heart to speak of it. One would need, for an apt analogy, to imagine a defeated right wing eagerly embroiled in discussions of the monarchy, the family, the death of chivalry and the possibility of reclaiming India, while maintaining a coy silence on what after all engages them most viscerally, the rights of property, since these had been so thoroughly expropriated that it seemed merely academicist to speak of them. With Darwinian conformity, much of the cultural left has taken on the colour of its historical environs: if we live in an epoch in which capitalism cannot be successfully challenged, then to all intents and purposes it does not exist. As for Marxism, Lenin was just an 'elitist', theory and political organization are 'male', and – a slight intellectual advance, this – historical progress is 'teleology' and any concern with material production 'economism'. As far as 'theory' goes, that the West is indeed now stuffed with brilliant young male zombies who know all about Foucault and not much about feeling is no reason for concluding that Julia Kristeva should have stuck to lyric poetry. A long time ago we fell into an obscure disaster known as Enlightenment, to be rescued around 1972 by the first lucky reader of Ferdinand de Saussure. The political illiteracy and historical oblivion fostered by much postmodernism, with its cult of flashy theoretical fashion and instant intellectual consumption, must surely be a cause for rejoicing in the White House, assuming that the trend does not pass out of existence before it reaches their ears.

None of this, however, implies that the politics of postmodernism are *nothing but* placeholders for a political desire which dare not speak its name. On the contrary, they represent not only questions of world-historical importance, but the appearance on the theoretical centre stage of millions who have been dumped and discarded, as often by traditional leftists as by the system itself. The claims of these men and women have figured not merely as a fresh set of political demands, but as an imaginative transfiguration of the very concept of the political. We would know that the dispossessed had really come to power when the word 'power' no longer meant what it used to. The paradigm shift which has accordingly been brought to birth – a veritable revolution in our conception of the relations between power, desire, identity, political practice – represents an immeasurable deepening of the fleshless, anaemic, tight-lipped politics of an earlier era. Any socialism which fails to transform itself in the light of this fecund, articulate culture will surely be bankrupt from the outset. Every one of its treasured concepts – class, ideology, history, totality, material production – will need to be thought through again, along with the philosophical anthropology which underpins them. The complicities between classical left-wing thought, and some of the dominative categories it opposes, have been embarrassingly laid bare. At its most militant, postmodernism has lent a voice to the humiliated and reviled, and in doing so has threatened to shake the imperious self-identity of the system to its core. And for this one might almost forgive it the whole of its egregious excesses.

The politics of postmodernism, then, have been at once enrichment and evasion. If they have opened up vital new political questions, it is partly because they have beat an undignified retreat from older political issues – not because these have disappeared or been resolved, but because they are for the moment proving intractable. In the early 1970s, cultural theorists were to be found discussing socialism, signs and sexuality; in the late 1970s and early 1980s they were arguing the toss over signs and sexuality; by the late 1980s they were talking about sexuality. This was not, need one say, a displacement from politics to something else, since language and sexuality are political to their roots; but it proved, for all that, a way of valuably reaching beyond certain classical political questions, such as why most people do not get enough to eat, which ended up by all but edging them from the agenda. Feminism and ethnicity are popular today because they are markers in the mind of some of the most vital political struggles we confront in reality. They are also popular because they are not necessarily anti-capitalist, and so fit well enough with a post-radical age. Post-structuralism, which emerged in oblique ways from the political ferment of the late 1960s and early 1970s, and which like some repentant militant became gradually depoliticized after being deported abroad, has been among other things a way of keeping warm at the level of discourse a political culture which had been flushed off the streets. It has also succeeded in hijacking much of that political energy, sublimating it into the signifier in an era when precious little subversion of any other sort seemed easily available. The language of subjectivity has at once ousted and augmented questions of political action and organization. Issues of gender and ethnicity have permanently breached the enclosure of the white male Western left, of whom the most that can be said is that at least we are not dead, and couched themselves for the most part in a rampantly culturalist discourse which belongs to precisely that corner of the globe. Pleasure has returned with a vengeance to plague a chronically puritanical radicalism, and has also figured as a cynical brand of consumerist hedonism. The body – so obvious, obtrusive a matter as to have been blandly overlooked for centuries – has ruffled the edges of a bloodless rationalist discourse, and is currently *en route* to becoming the greatest fetish of all.

It is maybe worth noting that the style of thought I am trying on here, traditionally known as the dialectical habit of mind, is not greatly in favour with postmodernists themselves. To try to think both sides of contradiction simultaneously is hardly their most favoured mode, not least because the concept of contradiction finds little place in their lexicon. On the contrary, for all its talk of difference, plurality, heterogeneity, postmodern theory often operates with quite rigid binary oppositions, with 'difference', 'plurality' and allied terms lined up bravely on one side of the theoretical fence as unequivocally positive, and whatever their antitheses might be (unity, identity, totality, universality) ranged balefully on the other. Before battle has been joined, these more disreputable-looking conceptual warriors have usually been subtly got at – tampered with, disabled or travestied in some way, so that the victory of the angelic forces is well-nigh assured. In its more refined philosophical reaches, postmodern theory acknowledges the mutual interdependence of terms like identity and non-identity, unity and difference, system and Other; but in terms of *sensibility* there is no doubt on which side its sympathies lie. Unlike most postmodernists, I myself am a pluralist about postmodernism, believing in postmodern fashion that there are different narratives to be told of postmodernism too, some of them considerably less positive than others.

For all its vaunted openness to the Other, postmodernism can be quite as exclusive and censorious as the orthodoxies it opposes. One may, by and large, speak of human culture but not human nature, gender but not class, the body but not biology, *jouissance* but not justice, post-colonialism but not the petty bourgeoisie. It is a thoroughly orthodox heterodoxy, which like any imaginary form of identity needs its bogeymen and straw targets in order to stay in business. It is not, on the whole, comfortable with producing statements like 'liberal humanism, for all its pathetic illusions, is in some respects an enlightened enough phenomenon compared with Attila the Hun'; instead, it prefers to save itself the labour of dialectical thought with utterances like 'F. R. Leavis was a reactionary', while turning in the next breath to denounce absolute judgements and totalizing claims. It knows that knowledge is precarious and self-undoing, that authority is repressive and monological, with all the certainty of a Euclidean geometer and all the authority of an archbishop. It is animated by the critical spirit, and rarely brings it to bear upon its own propositions. The intellectual history of Marxism is strewn with self-reflexive acts, as Marxists have sought to grasp something of the historical conditions of possibility of their own doctrines;

perilously beyond one's control, that there are no subjects sufficiently coherent to undertake such actions in the first place, that there is no total system to be changed in any case, that any apparently oppositional stance has already been pre-empted by the ruses of power, and that the world is no particular way at all, assuming we can know enough about it to assert even that?

But in seeking to cut the ground from under its opponents' feet, postmodernism finds itself unavoidably pulling the rug out from under itself, leaving itself with no more reason why we should resist fascism than the feebly pragmatic plea that fascism is not the way we do things in Sussex or Sacramento. It has brought low the intimidating austerity of high modernism with its playful, parodic, populist spirit, and in thus aping the commodity form has succeeded in reinforcing the rather more crippling austerities generated by the marketplace. It has unleashed the power of the local, of the regional and idiosyncratic, and has helped to homogenize them across the globe. Its nervousness of such concepts as truth has alarmed the bishops and charmed the business executives, just as its compulsion to place words like 'reality' in scare quotes unsettles the pious *Bürger* in the bosom of his family but is music to his ears in his advertising agency. It has floated the signifier in ways which cause the autocrats to reach for their banal certitudes, and in doing so found itself mimicking a society founded on the fiction of credit in which money spawns money as surely as signs breed signs. Neither financiers nor semioticians are greatly enamoured of material referents. It is stamped by a deep suspicion of the Law, but without its daunting presence would be bereft of its own deviations and transgressions, which are parasitic upon it. It is brimful of universal moral prescriptions – hybridity is preferable to purity, plurality to singularity, difference to self-identity – and denounces such universalism as an oppressive hangover of Enlightenment. Like any brand of epistemological anti-realism, it consistently denies the possibility of describing the way the world is, and just as consistently finds itself doing so. At once libertarian and determinist, it dreams of a human subject set free from constraint, gliding deliriously from one position to another, and holds simultaneously that the subject is the mere effect of forces which constitute it through and through. It has produced some original insights into Kant, along with a good deal of cant. It believes in style and pleasure, and commonly churns out texts which might have been composed by, rather than on, a computer.

I have claimed that there is no need to see the political narrative I am telling about postmodernism as reductionist; but it is certainly, in one of the term's several colliding senses, historicist, and this, too, postmodernists themselves would be unlikely to find acceptable. For postmodern theory is leery of linear tales, not least those in which it comes to figure itself as nothing more than an episode. It contrasts in this way with socialist theory, which is only too content to view itself as belonging to a particular age – that of capital itself – and will thankfully no longer need to stay in business when that era comes to a close, if it ever does. Socialists will then be released from the inconvenience of their beliefs, in which there is little profit and scant pleasure, and feel free to talk about something more enjoyable for a change, such as colour imagery in Joseph Conrad or the curiously mellow quality of Cotswold stone.

Postmodernism, by contrast, cannot really come to a conclusion, any more than there could be an end to post-Marie Antoinette. It is not, in its own eyes, an 'historical stage', but the ruin of all such stagist thought. It does not come after modernism in the sense that positivism comes after idealism, but in the sense that the recognition that the emperor has no clothes comes after gazing upon him. And so, just as it was true all along that the emperor was naked, so in a way postmodernism was true even before it got started. It is, at one level at least, just the negative truth of modernity, an unmasking of its mythical pretensions, and so was presumably just as true in 1786 as it is today. This is not an entirely comforting thought for postmodernism, since its historical relativism makes it wary of such transhistorical truths; but this claim is simply the price it has to pay for refusing to see itself, philosophically at least, as just another movement in the great symphony of History, one which evolves logically out of its predecessors and paves the way to what follows.

What postmodernism refuses is not history but History – the idea that there is an entity called History possessed of an immanent meaning and purpose which is stealthily unfolding around us even as we speak. There is then something rather paradoxical about declaring an end to this entity, since in doing so one inevitably embraces the logic one refuses. It would be rather like speaking of the moment when time began, or of imagining that something called eternity will commence at the point of one's death. If we can *date* an end to History – if postmodernism took off in the 1960s, or the 1970s, or whenever it was that Fordism or autonomous culture or metanarratives supposedly ground to a halt – then we are still to some extent within the framework of that linear tale. 'To some extent', since it is hard to know whether an ending is inside or outside whatever it wraps up, just as it is hard to know whether the border of a field is part of the field or not. But since an ending has to be the ending of something tolerably specific, an ending to *this* and not that, it is difficult not to feel that postmodernism grows out of modernism in much the same sense that modernism grew out of realism. The embarrassment of postmodernism in this respect is that, while culturally speaking it would indeed appear to have the look of a particular historical period about it, philosophically speaking it must have been true for a very long time, long before anybody had even heard of the signifier or circuits of libidinal intensity.

Is the 'post', then, an historical or a theoretical marker? If History as modernity conceives of it is just an illusion, then some postmodernist claims were surely true all along, even though it might be difficult to say who exactly they were true *for*. There never was any Progress or Dialectic or World-Spirit in the first place; this is not the way the world is, or ever was. But postmodern theory is shy of such phrases as 'the way the world is', or was; surely it is not contrasting 'ideological illusion' with 'the truth', in an epistemological move it would regard as intolerably naive? So perhaps it is the case that modernity, in its day, was real enough – that these notions of progress and dialectic and the rest really did have material effects, really did correspond in some way to a certain historical reality. But in that case postmodernism buys its immunity from epistemological naivety only at the cost of an historicism it finds equally distasteful. It also suggests that we are somehow superior to the past, which might offend its anti-elitist relativism.

This is why the idea of postmodernism as the *negative* truth of modernity is a necessary manoeuvre, since it allows one to reject modernity without claiming that you do so from some loftier vantage-point of historical development, which would of course be to fall prey to modernity's own categories. Postmodernism must indeed have some sense of how it is with the world, if it is to be able to claim that, say, Hegel was in many ways up a gum tree about it; but ideas of how it is with the world would appear to belong to a clapped-out Enlightenment rationality. The most crafty solution to this dilemma is a Nietzschean one: how the world is is *no way in particular*, and what is thus wrong with modernity is just the fact that it thinks there is an inherent shape to it all. Postmodernism is not delivering another narrative about history, just denying that history is in any sense story-shaped. The objection, in other words, is not to conceptually strait-jacketing history in this or that way, but to conceptually strait-jacketing it at all – rather as Michel Foucault objects to particular regimes of power not on moral grounds – for where would such criteria spring from in his theory? – but simply on the grounds that they are regimes as such, and so, from some vague libertarian standpoint, inherently repressive. (The more pessimistic side of Foucault, however, is far too disenchanted to endorse his own mad dreams of multiplicity.)

But there are problems with this objection to conceptual strait-jacketing as such. For one thing, it is not easy to see how we can *know* that history is no way in particular. We would surely have to be occupying quite an Olympian vantage-point to be certain of any such thing. For another thing, the case is suspiciously formalistic: is every attempt to force history into a particular mould just as noxious as every other? Civic humanism as much as fascism? This sounds implausible: one would seem to need some more finely nuanced grounds of discrimination, but it is not clear where they would spring from. Perhaps they could be derived in this way, which conjures a moral content out of a formal point: the world itself is just a ceaseless play of difference and non-identity, and whatever most brutally squashes all this is what is most reprehensible. So one could preserve one's ontology without the embarrassment of having to pretend that there was nothing to choose between Goethe and Goebbels.

But this resolves one problem only to throw up another. If difference and non-identity are just the way things are, which is to say no determinate way at all, and if this is a truth we would grasp if only we could shuck off our homogenizing concepts and levelling meta-languages, are we not landed back in some version of the naturalistic fallacy, which holds that there is a way of getting from the way things are to the way we should live, leaping from description to prescription? Postmodernism believes that politically speaking we should celebrate difference, plurality, the pied and dappled nature of our cultures, and some of it discerns an 'ontological' ground to all this in the world's not being any way in particular. This ontology then offers to ground your ethics or politics by suggesting that we should live as the world does, an ethical imperative which cannot itself be grounded. For why should the fact that there are supposedly no unities or identities in reality have any implications whatsoever for our conduct? Why should fact – more precisely, the fact that there aren't any unimpeachable facts – become value? There are, after all, plenty of moralists who have believed that we should act against the grain of the way they take the world to be.

Postmodernism, then, is wary of History but enthusiastic on the whole about history. To historicize is a positive move, and History only stands in its way. If postmodern theory really does believe that historicizing is *ipso facto* radical, then it is certainly mistaken. It assumes that historicizing belongs largely on the left, which is by no means the case. You do not need to tell the Edmund Burkes, Michael Oakshotts and Hans-Georg Gadamers of this world that events can only be understood in their historical contexts. For a whole lineage of liberal or right-wing thinkers, a sensitive attunement to historical context, to the cultural mouldings of the self, to the subliminal voice of tradition and the force of the local or idiosyncratic, has been a way of discrediting what they take to be the anaemic ahistorical rationality of the radicals. Burke's appeal to prescription, venerable custom and immemorial heritage is in this sense much the same as contemporary pragmatism's appeal to our received social practices, even if the former is thinking of the House of Lords and the latter of baseball and free enterprise. For both schools of thought, history – which comes down to something like 'the way we happen to do things and have done so for rather a long time' – is a form of rationality in itself, immeasurably superior to such jejune notions as universal freedom or justice. There is, to be sure, a more radical brand of postmodern historicism which textualizes institutions and unmasks repressive power; but it is hardly an original point that there is a good deal of disconcerting common ground between this historicism's nervousness of abstract theory, its affection for the wayward, deviant and offbeat, and its suspicion of grand narratives, and the commonplace methods of much conservative historiography. To imagine that historicizing is inherently radical is to imagine that all liberals or conservatives are anti-historical formalists, which along with being false is far too convenient a piece of straw-targeting. You can believe that Shakespeare expresses universal value while still believing that he would not have written as he did in 1745, thus combining universalism and historicism. There is no reason why an intelligent non-radical should refuse to look at phenomena in their historical context. She may jib at *reducing* phenomena to their historical contexts, but then so do almost all radicals except vulgar Marxists, who exist these days historicist thought has held to the power of historical *explanation*, holding that the point of restoring a phenomenon to its historical context is to shed some light on how and why it came about, and so to gain a deeper understanding of it. There are stronger and weaker versions of this genetic theory; but postmodernism, which harbours a Humean scepticism of causality in the first place, cannot really be content with any of them. They smack too much of a hierarchy of determinations, and so offend its ontological pluralism, imply a realist epistemology (the world is significantly stratified independently of our interpretations of it), and risk playing into the hands of the grand narrators. As a result, postmodernism escapes what it sees as one specious form of transcendentalism only to land up with another. In the good old historicist days, it was thought possible to give some sort of historical or genetic explanation of, say, beliefs and interests – to argue that these didn't just spring from nowhere or drop from outer space, but were motivated in complex ways by the history one belonged to, and had discernible functions within it. The various theories of ideology were one way of accounting for some of the causal relations between history and belief. One type of postmodernist tries to outflank this move by pointing out that this sort of historical theory is itself a belief, and so becomes part of the problem to which it considers itself a solution. This would be akin to claiming that my apology for my broken promise is perfectly useless because it is just another piece of language.

Anyhow, so the theory goes, we cannot get a grip on our beliefs or interests by examining their historical determinants, since, in a vicious epistemological circle, what counts for us as such determinants will itself be determined by our interests and beliefs. In fact we cannot get a critical fix on these things at all, any more than we could haul ourselves up by our own bootstraps, see ourselves seeing something or get a grip on our own bodies from the inside. The rationality which would offer to weigh up our beliefs from outside operates only within those beliefs, is itself a product of them, and so is a corrupt, flagrantly partisan sort of judge. As Bertolt Brecht once remarked: only someone inside a situation can judge it, and he's the last person who can judge. Since our interests, beliefs and discourses are what constitute us as subjects in the first place, we would simply disappear were we to try to hold them at arm's length for critical inspection. If we *were* able to examine ourselves in this way, there would be nobody left over to do the examining. As with much postmodern thought, this particular theory manages to reinforce a certain philosophical fantasy in the very act of rejecting it. It holds, just as firmly as Matthew Arnold, that all critical self-reflection must involve some sort of sublime disinterestedness, in which we would come somehow to distance ourselves from our own historical situatedness. It thus fails to see that a certain capacity for critical self-reflection belongs to the way the human animal belongs to its world – that this is not some phantasmal alternative to our material embeddedness, but constitutive of the way that humans, as opposed to beavers or beehive hairdos, are actually inserted into their environs. That they are able, within limits, to make something of what makes them, is the very index of their historicity, a mode of being possible only to a labouring, linguistic creature.

The assumption that any critique of interests must itself be disinterested shows just how mortgaged postmodernism still is to its metaphysical forebears. It is just that those forebears believed in the possibility of disinterestedness, whereas postmodernism does not; nothing has otherwise altered. If critique was indeed disinterested, why would anybody bother to practise it? If for postmodernism we can't subject our own interests and beliefs to a degree of radical criticism, this is because belief, or interest, or discourse, have now been raised to the kind of transcendental position once occupied by a universal subjectivity, and before that by various other disreputable-looking candidates for the post. It is interests which are now transcendental, self-validating, impervious to criticism, a position which is certainly in somebody's interests. They represent that which we can never get back behind, and there can thus be no question of enquiring after their historical roots. The concept of ideology, which has served as one way among many of accounting for the way in which what we believe is related to what we do, thus falls conveniently to the ground – conveniently, since this style of argument, which leaves our social beliefs and investments immune from all radical challenge, is precisely an ideological discourse in itself.[3]

This strong conventionalist theory sometimes includes in the category of 'beliefs' observational propositions which nobody could currently doubt, thus expanding the term 'belief' to the point of uselessness. I do not entertain the belief that I have hair on my head but none on my knees, since there is no way I could not believe it. As with the case that 'everything is an interpretation', or its leftist equivalent 'everything is political', this position cancels all the way through, flying from our grasp like an overstretched piece of elastic. Conventionalism is anti-foundational; but since its conventions can behave just as coercively as old-fashioned foundations, it is as though it has multiplied such foundations (since there are of course many sets of conventions) rather than abolished them. It offers to explain our behaviour by showing how it is governed by conventions, which is tantamount to saying that we do this because this is what we do, which is no explanation at all. It has little to say to those who ask why we do it, or whether we might not do something different for a change.

Note too that on this theory it is impossible to say what kind of world our discourse or beliefs are *about*, any more than those who regard the Grand Canyon or the human body as wholly 'constructed' are able to say what it is that is being constructed. For them, the question is bound to remain as much a mystery as crop circles are for those who lack a sense of humour. Since facts are themselves products of discourse, it would be circular to seek to check our discourse off against them. The world makes no input into our conversation, even if it is what we are conversing about. 'Don't interrupt! We're talking about you!' is the pragmatist's response to whatever feeble cheep the world might put out, like a couple of bossy parents discussing their cowed child. But since the case makes no whit of difference to our behaviour, it is just as idle to assert it as it is, in the eyes of those who reject the 'correspondence theory' of truth, to assert that our language somehow 'corresponds' to reality. It is really a regressive return to the Wittgenstein of the *Tractatus Logico-Philosophicus*, who held that, since our language 'gives' us the world, it cannot simultaneously pass comment on its relation to it. We cannot raise from within language the question of language's relation to the world, any more than we can jump on our own shadows or hold up a rope we are trying to climb. That relationship, which could be shown but not spoken, had therefore to lapse into mystical silence.

The later Wittgenstein came to renounce this remorselessly monistic view, acknowledging instead that language hooked onto the world in all sorts of different ways, some of them critical or judgemental and some of them not. Instead of thinking of 'language as a whole', he began to consider speech acts like 'Ow!' or 'Fire!', which related to the world in the sense that some bit of it provided the *reason* for them. One might also claim, though Wittgenstein himself would not, that some of our speech acts relate to the world in the sense that their effect or intention is to conceal, mystify, rationalize, naturalize, universalize or otherwise legitimate parts of it, and that this is the group of speech acts traditionally known as ideology. It has nothing to do with some imaginary opposite to absolute truth, a postmodern straw target if ever there was one. A postmodern semiotics which attends only to the way the signifier produces the signified, rather than also to these complex operations of the signifier upon it, simply conflates a variety of speech acts, with variable relations between signs and things, with a model of 'language in general' centred on its world-constitutive role. In this sense, postmodernism, whatever its pluralist credentials, has yet to advance decisively beyond the monism of the early Wittgenstein.

An historical story of sorts can nevertheless be told about the theories we are inspecting, which those theories themselves would no doubt dismiss out of hand as just another discourse on all fours with its own. There was a time, back in the days of classical liberal capitalism, when it was still thought possible and necessary to justify your actions as a good bourgeois by an appeal to certain rational arguments with universal foundations. There were still available certain common criteria of description and evaluation, by which you could elicit some persuasive grounds for your conduct. As the capitalist system evolves, however – as it colonizes new peoples, imports new ethnic groups into its labour markets, spurs on the division of labour, finds itself constrained to extend its freedoms to new constituencies – it begins inevitably to undermine its own universalist rationality. For it is hard not to recognize that there are now a whole range of competing cultures, idioms and ways of doing things, which the hybridizing, transgressive, promiscuous nature of capitalism has itself helped to bring into being. (We shall see later that it is one of the more glaring errors of postmodernism to forget that the hybrid, plural and transgressive are *at a certain level* as naturally coupled with capitalism as Laurel is with Hardy.) The system is accordingly confronted with a choice: either to continue insisting on the universal nature of its rationality, in the teeth of the mounting evidence, or to throw in the towel and go relativist, gloomily or genially accepting that it can muster no ultimate foundations to legitimate its activities.

The uptight conservatives take the former road, while the laid-back liberal pragmatists take the latter. If the former strategy is increasingly implausible, the latter is certainly perilous. For as we shall see in due course, the system cannot really dispense with its metaphysical foundations, however much it is continually to be caught eroding them by its own distinctly non-metaphysical operations. There are societies today which are among the most hard-headed, pragmatic places on earth and yet full of high-toned metaphysical rhetoric about God, Freedom, Nation and Family, of the kind few English politicians could get away with without acute embarrassment. And this is hardly a fortuitous conjuncture. If the anti-foundationalist road is perilous, however, it is so only to a degree – for in boldly kicking out the foundations from under one's own life-forms, one inevitably drags them out from beneath one's opponents' too. They can now no more finally ground their challenge to you than you can metaphysically copperplate your defence against them. Moreover, so you might claim, as long as their critique goes to work, as it must, on *your* categories, it is bound to be collusive with them, and so not really a fundamental critique at all. It is just a way of chipping into the conversation which is Western civilization from a mildly different angle. The only full-blooded critique would be one launched from another universe entirely, which would then challenge our own culture no more than the cawing of a rook. True radicalism, conveniently enough for the system itself, would be utterly unintelligible – a fact apparently overlooked by the CIA, who no doubt continue to take a professional interest in Noam Chomsky even though he occasionally utters propositions intelligible to Clint Eastwood. Radicals are not particularly thrown by being told that what they are trying to do is just part of the ongoing conversation of their civilizations, as long as they are allowed to go ahead and do it. This claim goes so far down as to disappear. They do not mind being informed that firing all pragmatist professors from the universities is just a move in the pragmatist game, and one would trust that the professors themselves would take it in the right spirit too.

In its post-imperial phase, and in a supposedly multicultural society, the system can no longer plausibly claim that its values are superior to those of others, simply – key postmodern term – different. There can be no real comparison between two sets of values, since this would presume a third sort of rationality within which they could all be encompassed, which is part of what is being denied. This, as Bernard Williams has pointed out, is in fact an utterly fallacious assumption;[4] it is not by virtue of some third language shared between them that we are able to translate English into Malay. But the move serves to swaddle the dominant system from any very searching criticism, at the same time as it serves to enhance its liberal credentials. The more conservative forms of postmodernism represent the ideology of those who believe that, if the system is to survive, truth must be sacrificed to practice, a move which would have been mystifying to Jefferson or John Stuart Mill but not in the least to Friedrich Nietzsche. Perhaps in this respect Pontius Pilate was the first postmodernist. But as this project can never really prosper, since to sacrifice the notion of truth altogether would be to disable some rather useful principles of social cohesion like religion and civic morality, the more radical forms of postmodernism are in business to turn their suspicion of truth *against* their rulers' continuing need for it as a form of social control. The irony is that in doing so, in insisting that truth is a function of power and desire, they sail hair-raisingly close to what their rulers hold *in practice*.

The choice with which the system is faced can be recast as one between two different conceptions of freedom. On the one hand lies the old-style model of the rational, autonomous subject, which corresponds fairly well to the more classical phase of liberal capitalism. This subject, which was as revolutionary in its day as it was deeply flawed, was never in fact all that securely founded, since its very autonomy tends to rip it from the world which might lend it some anchorage, leaving it rooted in nothing more solid than itself. It is for this reason that its euphoria is also a kind of nausea, as the Romantics were well aware. The freedom of the subject puts it tragically at odds with Nature; but if it is grounded in the sense of being integrated into the world, then this reinforces it in one way only to undermine it in another. History is on the side of the free subject, but only by gathering it to its bosom and so constraining its autonomy. Either the subject hangs vertiginously in the air, compelled in solitary self-confinement to legislate for itself, its inner freedom mysteriously at odds with its empirical determination; or it is buoyed up by a history which is itself an unfolding narrative of emancipation, but thereby risks being reduced to no more than an effect of it. It is a choice, more or less, between Kant and Hegel.

Then, somewhat later in the day, we stumble on a postmodern subject whose 'freedom' consists in a kind of miming of the fact that there are no longer any foundations at all, and who is therefore at liberty to drift, either anxiously or deliriously, in a universe which is itself arbitrary, contingent, aleatory. The world, so to speak, grounds this subject in its own very groundlessness, licenses its free-floatingness by its own gratuitous nature. This subject is free not because it is undetermined, but precisely because it is determined by a process of indeterminacy. The dilemma of freedom and foundation is thus 'resolved' – but only at the risk of eliminating the free subject itself. For it is hard to see that one can really speak of freedom here at all, any more than a particle of dust dancing in the sunlight is free. As far as any 'positive' doctrine of freedom goes, a world which really was random would not stay still long enough for me to realize my freedom, in the sense of taking the reasonably determinate steps involved in furthering my chosen projects. Freedom demands closure, a paradox which postmodernism seems reluctant to entertain. This is one reason why its idea of freedom is often enough the 'negative' conception of it espoused by classical liberalism, and just as full of holes. But at least for liberalism there was a subject coherent enough to count as the locus of that liberty; whereas if the postmodern subject is diffused by fortuitous forces, split open by a ceaseless play of difference, then there would seem nothing to which the idea of freedom could be attached. The effort to 'ground' the subject, as the effect of conflictive processes, risks emptying it out and striking all talk of freedom, positive or negative, entirely redundant. No sooner have women become autonomous subjects, in a reasonable rather than bugbearish sense of the term, than postmodernism sets about deconstructing the whole category.

So it is that some radical postmodernist politics work with notions of emancipation which some other postmodernist theory would seem to explode. For what stable identity is there to be emancipated? Is not the whole notion of emancipation just another variant of an inner/outer, expressive/repressive paradigm which has been long since deconstructed? Perhaps, then, emancipation would not be some sort of process or event, but would consist simply in recognizing how things really are with the subject, which is to say no way in particular – how it is, even now, 'free' in the sense of being diffuse, decentred, provisional, and how it is merely our metaphysical rage for order which frustrates this perception. It would seem, then, that we could be free simply by taking thought – by substituting a true conception of the self for a false one. But this not only involves an epistemology with which postmodernism feels less than comfortable; it also repeats, in rather more modish a guise, the traditional errors of philosophical idealism. Whatever is restricting the self, it is unlikely that simply changing our view of ourselves will wish it away, as the more radical currents of postmodernism are well enough aware. For these political trends, it is not changing one's mind which abolishes grand narratives, as though they would simply vanish if we were all to stop looking at them, but certain material transformations in advanced capitalism itself.

We can turn back, finally, to that ambiguous 'post' in the word 'postmodernism'. Which parts of modernity has postmodernism left behind? All of it? The notion of human equality along with the idea of historical progress? The emancipation of women as well as of the working class? The belief in individual freedom and conscience as well as in the sovereignty of Reason? Some bits of modernity, like the idea of revolution, seemed to have collapsed in theory but not in practice, as recent revolutionary events in Eastern Europe would testify. (It ought to be something of an embarrassment to postmodernism that, just as it was discarding the concepts of political revolution, collective subjects and epochal transformations as so much metaphysical claptrap, these things broke out where they had been least anticipated. It might, however, prove some consolation to these theorists that the revolutions in question quickly took a turn towards their own admired marketplace culture.) The doctrine of universal progress has taken a beating, but particular kinds of historical progress (the dismantling of apartheid, for example) still seem on the cards, and although this sort of emancipation has by no means been

3
Histories

History, as opposed to history with a small *h*, is for postmodernism a teleological affair. It depends, that is, on the belief that the world is moving purposefully towards some predetermined goal which is immanent within it even now, and which provides the dynamic of this inexorable unfurling. History has a logic of its own, and co-opts our own apparently free projects for its own inscrutable ends. There may be set-backs here and there, but generally speaking history is unilinear, progressive and deterministic.

There is no need to worry about how best to confront people who hold this belief, because there aren't any. Unless they are hiding out in caves somewhere, too shamefaced to come out, such people disappeared from the face of the earth a long time ago. They noticed that the twentieth century was rife with war, famine and death-camps, that none of the great utopian or Enlightenment ideals seemed any nearer to being realized, and glumly decided to take themselves off. It is true that, a long time ago, there used to be Whigs, Hegelians and Marxists who believed something along these lines, but it is very doubtful that Karl Marx (who maintained that he was not a Marxist) was one of them. Marx had nothing but scorn for the idea that there was something called History which had purposes and laws of motion quite independent of human beings. To imagine that Marxism is a teleology in *this* sense, which many postmodernists appear to do, is just as lurid a travesty as imagining that Jacques Derrida believes that anything can mean anything else, that nobody ever entertained an intention and that there is nothing in the world but writing.

Socialism does indeed posit a *telos* of a kind: the possibility of a more just, free, rational and compassionate social order. But so of course do radical postmodernists. Indeed some postmodernists seem to posit a teleology of a much more ambitious kind: the idea, for example, that the Enlightenment led inevitably to the concentration camps. But neither party believes that there is anything historically guaranteed about the goal of a more just society, or that it is somehow even now stealthily at work as the secret essence of the present. In any case, socialists are not as enamoured of historicizing as some seem to consider. We have seen one reason for this already: the fact that historicizing is by no means an inherently radical affair. But there is another more interesting reason for this socialist scepticism of history. One vein of postmodernism views history as a matter of constant mutability, exhilaratingly multiple and open-ended, a set of conjunctures or discontinuities which only some theoretical violence could hammer into the unity of a single narrative. This thesis is then often enough pushed to a wildly implausible extreme: Dante and De Lillo, encapsulated as they are in their discrete historical moments, share nothing in common worth mentioning. The impulse to historicize capsizes into its opposite: pressed to the point where continuities simply dissolve, history becomes no more than a galaxy of current conjunctures, a cluster of eternal presents, which is to say hardly history at all. We must understand Oliver Cromwell in his historical context, but what is to count as this context? Postmodernism, after all, insists that all contexts are fuzzy and porous. We ourselves are heirs to the history of which Cromwell was part, since the past is what we are made of.

The truth is that we (post)moderns do of course have an enormous amount in common with Sophocles or Savonarola, and nobody has ever taken leave to doubt it. The quarrel over the universal features of humanity cannot be about anything so flagrantly self-evident, but about how far such features *matter* – how far, for example, they figure significantly in the analysis of any specific historical situation. Does it really matter that Sophocles presumably had two ears like us, and can it throw any light on *Antigone*? It may not especially illuminate *Antigone*, but the fact that Sophocles had a form of body in common with us, a material form which has altered little in the course of human history, is surely a matter of the greatest moment. If another creature is able in principle to speak to us, engage in material labour alongside us, sexually interact with us, produce something which looks vaguely like art in the sense that it appears fairly pointless, suffer, joke and die, then we can deduce from these biological facts a huge number of moral and even political consequences. This, at least, is one sense in which we can derive values from facts, whatever David Hume may have thought. Because of the form of their bodies, we would know more or less what attitudes to these animals it was appropriate to take up, such as respect, compassion, not cutting off their feet for the fun of it and the like.

Of course we ought to take up such attitudes to non-human creatures too; but we would not consider them as potential marriage partners, co-authors or comrades in some political insurrection, unless we were living in one of the wackier regions of California. There are limits to the forms of life we could share with creatures materially different from us, which is presumably what Wittgenstein had in mind when he remarked that if a lion could speak, we would not be able to understand what he said. We can get something out of Sophocles's texts, as we could not out of the poetry of some unusually eloquent snail. If, on the other hand, we encountered a creature looking much like us but incapable of irony, then we might well suspect that it was some cunningly devised machine, unless once more we were living in certain areas of California. If animals can speak, labour, sexually reproduce themselves and so on, then they must, unlike non-speaking creatures who labour only with their bodies, be familiar with some form of politics, however rudimentary. They would be bound to have some sort of power-system to organize their labour and social life, forms of sexual regulation and so on, along with certain symbolic frames within which they represented all this to themselves.

But it is unfashionable at the moment to dwell too long on such facts, since it seems to stake too much upon biology while undervaluing the significance of culture. At a certain point in the 1970s, all concern with biology became 'biologistic' overnight, just as the empirical became empiricist and the economic economistic. Properly afraid of a vulgar reductionism, some strands of postmodernism responded to this danger by the rather more violent tactic of erasing the biological, and occasionally the economic, altogether. In speaking materially about culture, it began to speak culturally about the material, not least about that most obvious material bit of us, the body. It is ironic in this light that postmodernism should be both suspicious of the body as material and devoted to specificity, since for traditional thinkers like Aristotle and Aquinas, matter is precisely what individuates. What makes us different for this style of thought is not the 'soul', which for Aquinas is the form of the body and thus common to us all, but the fact that we are all unique lumps of stuff. As far as the undeniably universal aspects of the species go, postmodernism imagined that all talk of a common human nature must be both idealist and essentialist. It was probably right about the latter, but wrong, as I shall be arguing later, that this is necessarily a vice. It was mistaken, however, about the former, since the Marxian notion of species being is certainly a materialist version of human nature, far removed from the eternal verities of the heart. Postmodernists, in other words, entertained an idealist concept of human nature; it was just that they rejected it whereas the idealists endorsed it. In this as in other respects, they became the inverted image of their antagonists.

It is no disproval of such human universals to point out that all these features are differently constructed by different cultures. One has only to ask oneself *which* activities are differently constructed to find the universal question stubbornly reposing itself. Of course one can sometimes be mistaken about such common ground: we thought they were playing some game like cricket whereas they were actually trying to get it to rain. And there is no doubt that the idea of a universal humanity, in the degenerate sense that one's own cultural prejudices should hold global sway, has been one of the most brutal ways of crushing the otherness of others under one's heel that history has yet come up with. It has played a central role in a poisonous, sometimes exterminationist ideology, and the panic-stricken postmodern reaction to it is thus a generous sort of error. Nor does it necessarily follow from the doctrine that what human beings have in common over the centuries is the most *important* thing about them, which is precisely where the liberal humanists go wrong, even if language, sexuality, labour, law and politics are hardly trivial affairs. It is not the fact that King Lear can walk, some of the time at least, which allows the play to resonate with us. Anyway, one can always ask: important from what point of view? If we were pondering synaesthesia in the writings of Proust, then the fact that Proust was a human being is unlikely to be the pivot of our analysis. It is just that it is dogmatic of postmodernism to universalize its case against universals and conclude that concepts of a shared human nature are *never* important, not even, say, when it comes to the practice of torture.

In *over*historicizing, postmodernism also underhistoricizes, flattening out the variety and complexity of history in flagrant violation of its own pluralistic tenets. As Francis Mulhern has written:

> (The) tacit reduction of *history* to *change* – a kind of hyper-history . . . is the most understandable of polemical habits, but it perpetuates a confusing half-truth. History is also – and decisively, for its greater part – *continuity*. The historical process is differential: it is patterned by a plurality of rhythms and tempos, some highly variable, some very little so, some measured by clocks and calendars, others belonging to the practical eternity of 'deep time'. Historical structures and events . . . are thus necessarily complex in character, never belonging to a single mode (continuity/discontinuity) or

> temporality. Contexts are brief and narrow (a generation, a political crisis) but they are also long and wide (a language, a mode of production, sex-gender privilege), and all of these at once.[1]

Postmodernist history, by contrast, tends to be vivid but one-dimensional, squeezing out this stratified concept of time for the sake of the short run, the contemporary context, the immediate conjuncture. As T. S. Eliot puts it in *Four Quartets*, 'History is now and England', a proposition with which few postmodernists would rush to concur. But by what *ukase* is this always the most relevant temporality? Why is postmodernism so arrogantly assured that the *longue durée* is never the most significant? Marxism is rather more pluralistic on the issue, sometimes examining a specific historical conjuncture (*What Is To Be Done?*, *The Eighteenth Brumaire of Louis Bonaparte*), sometimes exploring the 'deep' or epochal time of a mode of production (*Capital*).

Perhaps postmodernists are afraid that an attention to grand narratives will collapse all little narratives into mere effects of them; but it is hard to see that the *Brumaire* simply 'reads off' the state of the French class struggle from the nature of capitalist production in general. For Marx, at least, the goal of analysis was not the general but the concrete; it is just that he recognized, along with Hegel and any sober thinker, that there was no way of constructing the concrete without general categories. Devotees of particularism should try doing without them for a while, an experiment which would need to include never opening their mouths. The phrase 'this indescribably awful pain of mine' is brimful with generalities. Perhaps postmodernists are suspicious of the idea of continuity (though they are sceptical of clean breaks as well) because it smacks of a falsely homogenizing habit of thought, raises the spectre of a revered tradition and carries with it a revoltingly smug implication of progress. In which case they should consider that there are emancipatory as well as oppressive traditions, and consider too this comment of Theodor Adorno: 'No universal history leads from savagery to humanitarianism, but there is one leading from the slingshot to the megaton bomb ... the One and All that keeps rolling on to this day – with occasional breathing spells – would teleologically be the absolute of suffering'.[2]

This remark of Adorno, delivered in the shadow of Auschwitz, brings us close to the heart of the socialist sense of history, whatever its author's own political heterodoxy. For socialist thought, there has indeed been a grand narrative, and more's the pity. It is a truth to be mourned rather than celebrated. It would be far better if the postmodernists were right, and there was nothing constant or continuous about the chronicle at all. But the price of believing this is a betrayal of the dead, along with a majority of the living. What strikes a socialist most forcibly about history to date is that it has displayed a most remarkable consistency – namely, the stubbornly persisting realities of wretchedness and exploitation. Of course these things have taken many different cultural forms. It is astonishing just how many ways of being deprived and dominated there are, quite enough to assuage the postmodernist's hunger for plurality. But if history really *were* wholly random and discontinuous, how would we account for this strangely persistent continuity? Would it not loom up for us as the most extraordinary coincidence – that a human history which according to some is just the ceaseless chance twist of the kaleidoscope should again and again settle its pieces into the patterns of scarcity and oppression? Why would it not be occasionally punctuated with episodes of peace and love? Why is there that in history which seems to resist definitive transformation, as a kind of internal drag or weighting? If history really is haphazard, and if there is, as the liberals would have it, a bit of good and bad in us all, then one would expect by the law of averages that history would from time to time have thrown up a few regimes which were morally exemplary, or at least morally creditable. But this has signally not happened. What most half-decent people would regard as virtue has never been in the political ascendancy, other than briefly and untypically. On the contrary, the political record of humankind has been appalling. From the moment they emerged upon the earth, human beings have systematically injured, plundered and enslaved one another. Our own century has been easily the bloodiest on record, which suggests that the idea of particular fallings-off no more necessarily implies a nostalgia for the good old days than a belief in particular types of progress is necessarily a triumphalist reading of history as a whole.[3] This is not of course to deny that there has also been a great deal of resplendent goodness, just that part of what we admire about that goodness is that it comes as something of a surprise. And most of it has belonged to the private rather than the public sphere.

This whole condition poses no problem for the Christian, who explains it with reference to original sin. But it ought to pose more of a theoretical challenge to the liberal or postmodernist than it seems to, assuming that they have bothered to reflect on the matter at all. How are we to account for this ceaseless din of hacking and gouging? If there is no way at all of accounting for it, then the misanthrope might well be right. If this is just the way it is with us, and the way it is likely to continue, then there is a real question as to whether human history is worth carrying on with. It is an academic question, of course, since history will carry on regardless, short of nuclear or environmental catastrophe; but whether the ha'pence outweigh the kicks is surely a debatable point. Certainly Schopenhauer considered it ludicrously self-deceiving to think that they did, believing as he did that it would have been far better for all concerned if someone had just blown the whistle some millennia ago and called the whole thing off. History, for the great majority of men and women who have lived and died, has been a tale of unremitting labour and oppression, of suffering and degradation – so much so that, as Schopenhauer had the courage to confess, it might well have been preferable for many people never to have been born at all. And for 'many', Sophocles would substitute 'all'.

If these are 'humanist' reflections, in the sense of thoughts concerning the species as a whole, they are hardly humanist in the more upbeat sense of the term, which suggests that 'humanism' and 'anti-humanism' are rather more nuanced concepts than many a postmodernist seems to assume. But it is hard in any case to imagine a style of thinking more alien to the postmodern sensibility. For postmodernism, as we have seen, does not typically concern itself with such embarrassingly transhistorical truths, nor until recently has it burdened itself overmuch with ethical questions; and the more debased brands of it are far too callow to speak of such matters as suffering, let alone on so sublime a scale. It is hard to imagine that Nirvana's publicity agents lost much sleep over the issue, though I may be doing them a grave injustice. If, however, postmodernism could be brought to discern some truth in this vision of humanity, how would it respond? That we should have faith that things might improve? This, one supposes, would smack rather too much of liberal progressivism to be wholly acceptable. For postmodernism, there is no singular 'thing' called history that could suffer either amelioration or decline; nor can it all be characterized in any dominant way, which is why I am seeking to embarrass postmodernism by claiming, with Adorno, that there has indeed been such a dominant mode right the way through. But the liberal progressive response is not acceptable from the liberal progressive either. For what possible evidence is there that this blood-stained history will take a turn for the better? On the contrary, almost all of the testimony is stacked against such wishful thinking. One can only have *reasonable* faith that this record might alter if one is able to account in some degree for its moral direness in non-moral terms – in terms, for example, of the kind of material conditions which bring about a permanent state of warfare, which give rise to an oppressive state and which make human exploitation the order of the day. There is no need to imagine that this would account for *all* human viciousness, or that it would relieve individual human beings of moral responsibility, or that changing these material conditions would produce a race of Cordelias. It is just a matter of recognizing that to be good you have to be well-heeled, even if to be too

which we might judge this condition are alienated along with us. A total alienation would cancel all the way through and appear to return us to where we were. History to date has been in some sense a set of extreme circumstances, as the dispossessed are aware and as the possessors are on the whole not; the states of emergency which are abnormal for the latter are routine for the former. But we could only know this if we had some idea already of what a non-extreme condition, one free from indignity and exploitation, would look like. And this could only spring from the very same history, which is one thing Marxists mean by describing that narrative as dialectical or self-contradictory.

To view that history as contradictory is to scotch the myth that Marxists are simple-minded devotees of progress, a fallacy which seems to have become stubbornly lodged in some postmodern minds. It is a mistake to believe that all grand narratives are progressive: Schopenhauer, perhaps the gloomiest philosopher who ever lived, was certainly much taken by one. But to argue against History as progressive is not, of course, to claim that there is never any progress at all – a vastly implausible belief which postmodernism at its most cynical would nonetheless seem to entertain. You do not need to believe in a golden age to hold that the past was in some respects better than the present, just as you do not need to be an odiously self-satisfied Whig to argue that the present is in some respects better than the past. These are empirical rather than metaphysical judgements, which have in mind such things as the benefits of modern anaesthetics or of a nuclear-free medieval Europe. Nobody in this sense disbelieves in historical progress, and anyone who did would be making quite as meta-narrational a claim as someone who thought that history has been steadily on the up since the sack of Rome. But this is different from believing that, say, there is a universal pattern to history characterized by an inexorable growth of productive forces. Certainly Marx did not believe this; on the contrary, he seems to have thought that stagnation rather than development was the more typical condition. Marxism is not a brand of technological determinism which holds, for example, that the various historical modes of production must follow on from each other in some rigidly mechanistic way.

As far as the notion of universal historical progress goes, then, there would seem nothing to choose between Marxism and postmodernism. The difference lies in the fact that, when it comes to the modern epoch, Marxism is rather more nuanced than some postmodernism about how progressive or otherwise it is. Some radical postmodernism tends to be pluralistic about political opposition but monistic about the system which it confronts. As we have seen, this style of thought sometimes sees the dominant system itself as just 'oppressive', and looks for positive value to what it has sidelined. Its politics are thus a classsic instance of the binary thinking it otherwise sees fit to chide. It takes this simplistic view of the dominant power partly because, as we have seen, it flirts with the naive libertarian belief that power, system, law, consensus and normativity are themselves unequivocally negative. If some postmodern philosophy takes a more subtle view, what one might call the general culture of postmodernism, its intuitive impulses and habits of feeling, does not. Words like 'norm', 'Law', 'authority', 'power' echo somewhat ominously in its collective consciousness. But power and authority are of course excellent things; it all depends on who has them in what circumstances for which purposes. The power to undo wretchedness is to be celebrated rather than derided, and the power to undo it absolutely is absolutely to be celebrated. Normativity is to be condemned if it means sexual strait-jacketing, but defended if it means, say, the routine agreement by which workers have a right to withdraw their labour in certain situations.

One reason why postmodernism instinctively suspects power as negative[4] is that the forms of power which most engage its attention are exactly that. There was never a good word to be said for patriarchy or racial supremacism. And it would then seem logical to extend this point to social class too, in so far as postmodernism can muster any enthusiasm for the notion. Social class tends to crop up in postmodern theory as one item in the triptych of class, race and gender, a formula which has rapidly assumed for the left the kind of authority which the Holy Trinity occasionally exerts for the right. The logic of this triple linkage is surely obvious: racism is a bad thing, and so is sexism, and so therefore is something called 'classism'. 'Classism', on this analogy, would seem to be the sin of stereotyping people in terms of social class, which taken literally would mean that it was politically incorrect to describe Donald Trump as a capitalist. Socialists, however, churlishly refuse to subscribe to the orthodoxy that social class is a bad thing, even though they are out to abolish it. For socialism, the working class is an excellent thing, since without it one could never usurp the power of capital. The bourgeoisie may be on the whole a bad thing today, but it was much to be admired in its revolutionary heyday, when it fought with remarkable courage against the brutalities of the *anciens régimes* and bequeathed us a precious inheritance of liberty, justice and human rights, not to speak of a magnificent culture. (It is this culture, incidentally, which many working men and women, as well as many colonial subjects, have set out painfully to acquire so as to turn it to their own ends, and which for some postmodernists can simply be junked.) The point, anyway, is that this is a rather different way of seeing from the kind of ahistorical moralism which holds that social class, like salt and smoking, is not very nice.

On the surface, the class–race–gender triplet appears convincing enough. Some people are oppressed because of their gender, some on account of their race, and others by virtue of their class. But this is a deeply misleading formulation. For it is not as though some individuals display certain characteristics known as 'class', which then result in their oppression. On the contrary, Marxists have considered that to belong to a social class just *is* to be oppressed, or to be an oppressor. Class is in this sense a wholly social category, as being female or having a certain skin pigmentation is not. These things, which are not to be mistaken for being feminine or African American, are a matter of the kind of body you have rather than the sort of culture you belong to. Nobody who is aware of the sorry pass to which culturalism has brought us could doubt the need to assert anything so starkly self-evident.[5] It is the kind of statement that postmodernists tend to find acutely problematic, since they assume with breathtaking dogmatism that all reference to Nature, in human affairs at least, is treacherously 'naturalizing'. The natural, on this view of it, is just a mystifying word for those questionable cultural practices we have come to take for granted. It is easy to see how this applies to the view that human civilization would collapse without the St Patrick's day parade, but harder to see how it applies to events like breathing and bleeding. It is not even true that 'naturalizing' applies to all ideology, as almost everyone from Georg Lukács to Roland Barthes seems to have assumed.[6] Postmodernism itself inveighs against 'naturalizing' while itself sometimes absolutizing the present system. It lays rhetorical claim to the title of 'materialist' and then, understandably wary of racist or sexist biologisms, proceeds to suppress the most obviously materialist part of human beings, their biological make-up.

As a result, this brand of culturalism is bound to miss what is peculiar about those forms of oppression which move at the interface of Nature and culture. The oppression of women is a matter of gender, which is wholly a social construct; but women are oppressed *as women*, which involves the kind of body one happens to have. Being bourgeois or proletarian, by contrast, is not a biological affair at all. There will be no bourgeoisie or proletariat in an emancipated society, though there will certainly be women and Celts. There can be liberated women, in the sense of individuals who are both female and emancipated, but there cannot be liberated wage-slaves in the sense of people who are both at the same time. 'Industrial middles class' and 'proletarian' are entirely relational matters, in the sense that no society could have one without the other; but sexual and ethnic categories are not wholly mutually constitutive in this way. Masculine and feminine, like Caucasian and African American, are most certainly mutually defining categories. But nobody has one sort of skin pigmentation because someone else has another, or is male because someone else is female, in the sense that some people are only landless labourers because others are gentlemen farmers.

In any case, Marxism is not definitively to do with class at all. As Marx himself once commented, what was original about his and Engels's thought was not the discovery of social class, which had been as obvious as Mont Blanc long before they came to write. It was the more controversial claim that the birth, flourishing and demise of social classes, along with the struggles between them, are bound up with the development of historical modes of material production. This may or may not be true, but it is important to get straight what one's interlocutors are actually saying. It is this historical perspective which distinguishes Marxism from those critiques of class which attend only to its more oppressive effects in the present. Marxism is not just a high-sounding way of finding it distasteful or 'privileged' that some people belong to one social class and some to another, as it might be thought objectionable that some get to attend cocktail parties while others have to make do with a can of beer from the icebox. Marxism is a theory of the role played by the conflict between social classes in a much wider process of historical change, or it is nothing. And on this theory, social class cannot be said to be unequivocally a bad thing, and so conflated with racism and sexism. It is only a postmodernist oblivion of the many-sidedness of history which could license such a manoeuvre in the first place.

There is another possible error encouraged by the race–class–gender triplet. What these social groups have in common is the fact that in present conditions they are denied their full humanity – though most postmodernists would be suspicious of the phrase 'full humanity', and some of them, for that matter, of the word 'humanity'. But socialism's interest in working people is not in the first place a question of any such moral judgement. Working people are not the potential agents of socialist democracy because they suffer a good deal. As far as misery goes, there are a good many more promising candidates for political agency: vagrants, poor peasants, prisoners, senior citizens, even impoverished students. Socialists have nothing against these groups; indeed some of them have been impoverished students or even prisoners themselves, and if the young persist with their post-political apathy it is probable that all socialists will soon be senior citizens. But these groups are not even potential agents of socialist change, since they are not so located within the system of production, so organized by and integral to it, as to be capable of running it more cooperatively. It is not a matter of competition between socialists and postmodernists as to which oppressed group should be swooped in upon and most vigorously promoted, since as far as socialism is concerned there can be no choice in the matter. Since nobody can accomplish anyone else's emancipation for them, it is a question of democratic principle that those victimized by an oppressive power must free themselves from it; and in the area of material production, this means those who are most directly disadvantaged by it. But it follows from the same principle that, for example, women, and not working people as such, are the agents of political change when it comes to the sway of patriarchy. If it is a mistake of some Neanderthal Marxists to imagine that there is a single agent of social transformation (the working class), it is equally an error of new-fangled postmodernists to imagine that this agent has now been outdated by the 'new political movements'. For this would mean either denying that economic exploitation exists, or imagining with 'elitist' presumption that women or gays or ethnic groups who were not part of the working class could substitute themselves for it in challenging the power of capital.

Socialists, then, are not quite so absolutist in their attitudes to social class as relativistically minded postmodernists; nor do they view the prevailing social system in such reductive, monological terms. It is true that not all postmodernism does so either: some of it, for example, guardedly applauds consumerist freedom while remaining critical of capitalism in other ways. But this weighing of empirical gains and losses is rather different from a grasp of the system's historically contradictory nature. Is the capitalist system progressive? The only reasonable answer is a firm yes and no. On the one hand, Marx's praise for capitalism is surely well justified. Capitalism, as he never tires of arguing, is the most dynamic, revolutionary, transgressive social system known to history, one which melts away barriers, deconstructs oppositions, pitches diverse life-forms promiscuously together and unleashes an infinity of desire. Typified by surplus and excess, constantly overriding the measure, it is a mode of production which breeds a hitherto undreamt-of wealth of human energies, bringing the individual to a peak of subtle complexity. As the greatest accumulation of productive forces which history has ever witnessed, it is capitalism which for the first time makes feasible the dream of a social order free of want and toil. As the first truly global mode of production, it uproots all parochial obstacles to human communication and lays down the conditions for international community. Its political ideals – freedom, justice, self-determination, equality of opportunity – outshine, in principle at least, almost all previous ideologies in the depth of their humanism and the universality of their scope.

All of this, of course, is bought at the most terrible cost. This dynamic, exuberant release of potential is also one long unspeakable human tragedy, in which powers are crippled and squandered, lives crushed and blighted, and the great majority of men and women condemned to fruitless labour for the profit of a few. Capitalism is most certainly a progressive system, and is just as certainly nothing of the kind. And it is Marxism which is reproached by postmodernism for its monistic, reductive, unilinear vision! The image which Marxism offers of capitalism is that of a system frozen in its fixed modes of representation, yet mobilizing a desire which overturns all representation; which gives birth to a great carnival of difference, inversion, transgression, while never ceasing to be rigidly self-identical; which reproduces itself by a rigorously quantified exchange of commodities which are spectral and elusive, incarnate conundrums of presence and absence; which constantly conjures material inequality out of abstract equality;

which is in need of an authority it continually flouts, and of immutable foundations it threatens to kick away; and which ceaselessly presses up against its own limits and nourishes its own antagonists. It is no wonder that irony was one of Marx's most treasured tropes.

Capitalism, in short, itself deconstructs the difference between system and transgression, in however partial a mode; and it is the language of historical materialism which has traditionally set out to capture this well-nigh unthinkable set of aporias. The idea of a system whose very logic sets it askew to itself: this, surely, was implicit in historical materialism long before deconstruction arrived on the intellectual agenda. It is this dialectical vision which refuses on the one hand the kind of reactionary postmodernism for which the marketplace can be viewed as enthrallingly positive, and on the other hand the kind of radical postmodernism for which creative value must be found, not secreted in the very logic of the system itself, but only in its fissures or waste products, on its peripheries or in its apocalyptic negations. Both ways of thinking miss, from different directions, the aporetic nature of capitalism, the mind-bending paradox of a system whose margins are installed at its centre.

To claim that the capitalist system constantly presses up against its own limits is another way of saying that the project of modernity is a self-marring one. Much of the socialist project, one might venture, really boils down to a single *faux naïf* question addressed to liberal Enlightenment: Why is it that its splendid ideals can never be realized in practice? Under what material conditions does it come about that, as soon as these admirable notions of freedom, justice and the rest descend from heaven to earth, from the sphere of ideology to that of political society, they begin to twist by some inexorable logic into their opposites? Might this, for example, have to do with the fact that the realization of individual freedom in the economic sphere then ends up undermining freedom (along with justice and equality) in society as a whole? Might not the anarchy of the marketplace necessarily breed an authoritarian state? Might not the forms of instrumental reason needed to control a hostile environment also be used to shackle and suppress human beings themselves?

If all this is true, then there is a sense in which modernity as a project never really got off the ground. Or rather, it unfurled its triumphal course only to unravel its own progress at every point. And this is then one way of accounting for the growth of postmodernism, which springs among other sources from the impossibilities of modernity, from its implosion or ironic self-scuppering. But this was an impossibility which was inherent in it all along, not some final collapse which then allows postmodernism to get off the ground. It is the idealism of postmodernism's riposte to modernity with which socialism takes issue, its occasional assumption that this mighty historical epoch is no more than a set of spurious notions and chimerical narratives, its failure to raise the question of the specific historical conditions under which fine ideas like reason or freedom or justice are bound to become pathetic travesties of themselves. It is to these *necessary* contradictions of modernity that socialism addresses itself, not just to some purely formal question of the viability or otherwise of grand narratives. For if *this* particular grand narrative failed, it was not just for epistemological reasons, but because – for example – liberal theory posits a universality which liberal practice just as surely undermines, or because liberty for some in such conditions is inseparable from unfreedom for others. None of this establishes the bankruptcy of grand narratives as such, simply the tragedy of a history whose ideals were bound to ring hollow to its inheritors because it was structurally incapable of giving them flesh. Postmodernism is in some sense the Oedipal child of that age, squirming with embarrassment at the gap between the big talk of the father and his feeble deeds. Because bourgeois society is a puny patriarch, incapable of universalizing its ideas of freedom or justice or autonomy, its very conception of the universal becomes corrupted by this fact. But this is different from arguing that universality is specious as such – a move which pays modernity the extravagant compliment of having defined the concept in the only possible way. There is little to be gained by replacing the abstract assertion of universality with the equally abstract rejection of it.

In the end, though, socialism and postmodernism are not irreconcilably at odds on the question of history. Both believe in a history which would be one of plurality, free play, plasticity, open-endedness – which would not, in a word, be History. For Marx, the aim is to release the sensuous particularity of use-value from the metaphysical prison of exchange-value, which implies a great deal more than economic change. It is just that the two outlooks differ over how this desirable goal of plurality is to be attained. For the more brittle currents of postmodernism, that history can be had right now, in culture, discourse, sex or shopping mall, in the mobility of the contemporary subject or the multiplicities of social life. This false utopianism projects the future into the present, thus selling the future short and imprisoning the present within itself. But it is right to see that unless a feasible future *were* somehow discernible within the present, unless we can point to what current freedoms and fulfilments might give it shape, the idea of the future remains bloodlessly abstract, which is another kind of false utopia. The drastic prematurity of postmodernism is also a rebuke to that grim-lipped deferment of happiness at which the traditional male left has been so depressingly adept.

For a less compromised variety of postmodernism, to exist historically is to break through the falsifying schema of History and live dangerously, decentredly, without ends or grounds or origins, letting rip the odd snarl of sardonic laughter and dancing ecstatically on the brink of the abyss. It is hard to know what this would mean in practice – how exactly would one live 'decentredly' in Chipping Norton, and whether dancing on the brink of the abyss is compatible with, say, wearing horn-rimmed spectacles or returning one's library books on time. Those who celebrate the discontinuous subject, which includes, by the way, a good many of the empiricists postmodernism denounces, would no doubt be as perturbed as the rest of us if their children failed to recognize them from week to week, or if their philosophically minded bank manager refused them the money they had deposited six months ago on the grounds that it could no longer be said to be theirs. It is also hard to see how this view is not just another form of idealism, for which freedom resides in reading the world differently. For a more radical vein of postmodernism, freedom and plurality are still to be politically created, and can be achieved only by struggling against the oppressive closure of History, the material conditions for which have now been laid down by radical transformations in the system itself. Socialism, as we have seen, would agree with combating History: it has no particular desire to perpetuate a grand narrative which has been on the whole one of hardship and indignity. It is just that it disagrees that the system has transformed itself to the point where socialists are likely to get enough of what they want, or no longer need some of what they traditionally required.

Marx himself refused to dignify everything that had happened so far with the title of history. For him, it had all been 'pre-history', one tedious variation after another on the abiding motif of exploitation. And this 'pre-history' is akin in some ways to the postmodernist's History. It is, as both Marx and Joyce's Stephen Dedalus comment, a 'nightmare' from which we are trying to awaken; but to dream that one has awoken only to discover that one hasn't is just more of the nightmare, and a suitable image of postmodern prematurity. For socialism, the death of History is still to arrive, not a brisk dispatching of the past which could come about right now, perhaps by reading Fukuyama or Jean-François Lyotard, and which would allow us to start afresh. Few themes have a more venerable historical pedigree than the idea that we can break with history. And as Ellen Wood points out, epistemological scepticism has a history as old as philosophy itself.[7] The point for Marx is not to move us towards the *telos* of History, but to get out from under all that so that we may make a beginning – so that histories proper, in all their wealth of difference, might get off the ground. This, in the end, would be the only 'historic' achievement. And here universality and plurality go hand in hand. For only when the material conditions exist in which all men and women can be freely self-determining can there be any talk of genuine plurality, since they will all naturally live their histories in different ways. Only when we have the institutional means of determining our own histories will we cease to be constrained by History. In this sense, the humanist notion of the self-determining agent, and the postmodern conception of the multiple subject, are not finally at odds. But they are at odds for us *now* – since to bring about those conditions would involve instrumental action, determinate purposes, ideas of truth, precise forms of knowledge, collective subjectivities, the sacrifice of certain pleasures – in short, all that the more consumerist forms of postmodernism finds most distasteful.

This is yet another sense in which for socialism history moves under the sign of irony. And it is a dangerous irony too, since it is easy enough to destroy the non-instrumental goal in the instrumental pursuit of it, to justify the functional means by the non-functional end. To this extent, those who wish to locate utopia in the present at least remind us of what we are fighting for, even if they also help to defer its realization. The goal of socialism is to fashion a society in which we would no longer have to justify our activities at the tribunal of utility – in which the realization of our powers and capacities would become a self-delighting end in itself. Marx believes that such free self-realization is a kind of absolute moral value, though he is of course aware that what powers and capacities we actually have, and how we realize them, are historically specific. This is another sense in which universality and particularity are not for him ultimately at odds, even if they split apart in the commodity or in the rift between state and civil society. Socialism is thus at root an aesthetic matter: where art was, there shall humans be. But there are different ways of aestheticizing social existence, and this one is rather different from lifestyle, design, the commodity or the society of the spectacle.

The quarrel here between socialists and postmodernists revolves in part on the concept of 'closure'. Postmodernists tend to be nervous of the notion, identifying it as they do with objectionable forms of dogmatism and exclusiveness. But dogma and closure are not synonymous. 'Dogma' in the pejorative sense does not mean utterances which are 'closed', since what utterances are not, but truth-claims which refuse to summon any reasonable grounds or evidence for themselves. In this sense, one of the commonest forms of postmodernist dogma is an intuitive appeal to 'experience', which is absolute because it cannot be gainsaid. (Not all appeals to experience need be of this kind.) Such intuitionism is the most subtle, pervasive form of contemporary dogmatism, far more prevalent in 'theoretical' circles than any authoritarian hectoring. There is also, one should remind post-structuralists in particular, a neutral sense of the term 'dogma', meaning simply that which is taught or promulgated, with no necessary implication that it is beyond rational contestation.

The point, anyway, is that some postmodern radicals detest the idea of closure so cordially that they would wish to exclude nobody whatsoever from their desired social order, which sounds touchingly generous-hearted but is clearly absurd. Closure and exclusion, for radical thought, are by no means to be unequivocally censured in some sentimental liberal spirit. There can by definition be no place for racists, exploiters or patriarchs in a free society, which is not to suggest that they should be hung by their heels from the church towers. A genuinely pluralist society can only be achieved by a resolute opposition to its antagonists. Failing to appreciate this is to project a pluralist future back into the conflictive present, in the manner of some postmodern thought, and thereby to risk stymieing that future altogether. The idea that all closure is oppressive is both theoretically sloppy and politically unproductive – not to speak of entirely idle, since there could be no social life without it. It is not a question of denouncing closure as such, a universalist gesture if ever there was one, but of discriminating between its more enabling and more disabling varieties. The postmodern hostility to closure is in some ways just a fancy theoretical version of the liberal disdain for 'labels' and 'isms'. It is characteristic of liberalism to find names and

4

Subjects

The postmodern subject, unlike its Cartesian ancestor, is one whose body is integral to its identity. Indeed from Bakhtin to the Body Shop, Lyotard to leotards, the body has become one of the most recurrent preoccupations of postmodern thought. Mangled members, tormented torsos, bodies emblazoned or incarcerated, disciplined or desirous: the bookshops are strewn with such phenomena, and it is worth asking ourselves why.

Sexuality, as Philip Larkin announced, began in the 1960s, partly as an extension of radical politics into regions they had lamentably neglected. But as revolutionary energies were gradually rolled back, a concern with the body came gradually to take their place. Erstwhile Leninists were now card-carrying Lacanians, and everyone shifted over from production to perversion. The socialism of Guevara gave way to the somatics of Foucault and Fonda. In the high Gallic pessimism of the former, as opposed to his more politically activist features, the left could find a sophisticated rationale for its own political paralysis. The fetish, for Freud, is that which plugs an intolerable gap; and there is a case for claiming that sexuality has now become the most fashionable fetish of all. The discourse which first launched the notion of sexual fetishism in a grand way has itself become a shining example of it. From Berkeley to Brighton, there's nothing more sexy than sex; and a concern for physical health has now escalated into a major neurosis. Conservatives have often of course proved obsessive on the topic of sexuality, viewing morality as about adultery rather than armaments, sexual deviancy rather than starvation; and one wonders if some postmodernists are not turning into a ghastly mirror-image of them.

The body, then, has been at once a vital deepening of radical politics, and a wholesale displacement of them. There is a glamorous kind of materialism about body talk, which compensates for certain more classical strains of materialism now in dire trouble. As a stubbornly local phenomenon, the body fits well enough with postmodern suspicions of grand narratives, as well as with pragmatism's love affair with the concrete. Since I know where my left foot is at any particular moment without needing to use a compass, the body offers a mode of cognition more intimate and internal than a now much-scorned Enlightenment rationality. In this sense, a *theory* of the body runs the risk of self-contradiction, recovering for the mind just what was meant to deflate it. But if the body provides us with a little sensuous certitude in a progressively abstract world, it is also an elaborately coded affair, and so caters also to the intellectual's passion for complexity. It is the hinge between Nature and Culture, offering surety and subtlety in equal measure. Indeed it is remarkable how the epoch of postmodernity has been characterized at once by a veering away from Nature and a sharp swing towards it. On the one hand everything is now cultural; on the other hand we must redeem a damaged Nature from the hubris of civilization. These apparently opposed cases are in fact secretly at one: if ecology repudiates the sovereignty of the human, culturalism relativizes it away.

For the philosophers and psychologists, mind is still a sexy notion; but literary critics have always been wary of the unhoused intellect, preferring their concepts to come fleshed and incarnate. In this sense, if by no means in others, the new somatics represents the return in a more sophisticated register of the old organicism. Instead of poems as plump as an apple, we now have texts as material as an armpit. This turn to the body sprang partly from a structuralist hostility to consciousness, and represents the final expulsion of the ghost from the machine. Bodies are ways of talking about human subjects without going all sloppily humanist, avoiding that messy interiority which drove Michel Foucault up the wall. For all its carnivalesque cavortings, body talk is thus, among other more positive things, our latest form of repression; and the postmodern cult of pleasure, at least in its Parisian varieties, is a very solemn, high-toned affair indeed.

For the new somatics, not any old body will do. If the libidinal body is in, the labouring body is out. There are mutilated bodies galore, but few malnourished ones. The finest body book of our era is surely Maurice Merleau-Ponty's *The Phenomeology of Perception*; but this, with its humanist sense of the body as practice and project, is for some thinkers distinctly *passé*. The shift from Merleau-Ponty to Foucault is one from the body as subject to the body as object. For Merleau-Ponty, as we have seen, the body is 'where there is something to be done'; for the new somatics, the body is where something – gazing, imprinting, regulating – is being done to you. It used to be called alienation, but that implies the existence of an interiority to be alienated, a proposition about which some postmodernism is deeply sceptical.

It is part of the damage done by a Cartesian tradition that one of the first images the word 'body' brings to mind is that of a corpse. To announce the presence of a body in the library is by no means to allude to an industrious reader. Thomas Aquinas thought that there was no such thing as a dead body, only the remains of a living one. Christianity places its faith in the resurrection of the body, not in the immortality of the soul; and this is just a way of saying that if heaven does not involve my body, it doesn't involve me. The Christian faith has of course much to say of the soul too; but for Aquinas the soul is the 'form' of the body, as wedded to it as the meaning is to a word. It was a point taken up by the later Wittgenstein, who once remarked that the body was the best image we had of the soul. Soul talk was necessary for those faced with a mechanical materialism which drew no real distinction between the human body and a banana. Both, after all, were material objects. In this context, you needed a language which sought to capture what distinguished the human body from the things around it, and soul talk at its best was a way of doing this. It easily backfired, however, since it is well-nigh impossible not to picture the soul as a ghostly sort of body, and so simply find yourself slipping a fuzzy object inside a grosser one as a way of accounting for the latter's uniqueness. But the human body does not differ from jam jars and toothbrushes because it secretes a spectral entity they lack; it differs from them because it is a centre from which they can be organized into significant projects. Unlike them, it is, as we say, creative; and if we had had a language which adequately captured this bodily creativity we would perhaps never have needed soul talk in the first place.

What is special about the human body, then, is just its capacity to transform itself in the process of transforming the material bodies around it. It is in this sense that it is anterior to those bodies, a kind of 'surplus' over and above them rather than an object to be reckoned up alongside them. But if the body is a self-transformative practice, then it is not identical with itself in the manner of corpses or carpets, and this is a claim that soul language was also trying to make. It is just that such language locates this non-self-identity in the body's having an invisible extra which is the real me, rather than viewing the real me as a creative interaction with my world – an interaction made possible by the peculiar kind of body I have. Stoats and squirrels cannot be said to have souls, however winsome we may find them, because their bodies are not of the kind that can work in complex ways upon the world and so necessarily enter into linguistic communion with their fellows. Soulless bodies are those that do not speak, or at least which do not sign. The human body is that which is able to make something of what makes it, and to this extent its paradigm is that other mark of our humanity, language, a given which continually generates the unpredictable.

It is important to see, as postmodernism largely does not, that we are not 'cultural' rather than 'natural' creatures, but cultural beings by virtue of our nature, which is to say by virtue of the sorts of bodies we have and the kind of world to which they belong. Because we are all born prematurely, unable to look after ourselves, our nature contains a yawning abyss into which culture must instantly move, otherwise we would quickly die. And this move into culture is at once our splendour and our catastrophe. Like all the best Falls it was a fortunate one, a fall up into civilization rather than one down to the beasts. The linguistic animal has the edge over its fellow creatures in all kinds of ways: it can be sardonic or play the trombone, torture children and stockpile nuclear weapons. Language is what emancipates us to a degree from the dull constraints of our biology, enabling us to abstract ourselves from the world (which includes for this purpose our bodies), and so to transform or destroy it. Language liberates us from the prison-house of our senses, and becomes an entirely weightless way of carrying the world around with us. Only a linguistic animal could have history, as opposed to what one imagines for a slug is just the same damn thing over again. (I have no wish to be patronizing here: no doubt slugs are marvellously intelligent beings in their own way, and probably make wonderful companions, but their existence, viewed from the outside, appears a trifle boring.) Because it has language, the human animal is in danger of developing too fast, unconstrained by its sensuous responses, and so of overreaching itself and bringing itself to nothing. Human existence is thus exciting but precarious, whereas the career of a slug is tedious but secure. Slugs and beavers cannot lunge at each other with knives, unless they are doing it on the quiet, but neither can they practise surgery. A creature condemned to meaning is an animal continually at risk. It belongs to our nature that we are able to go beyond it, as it belongs to the system of language that it is able to generate events known as speech acts which can transgress the system itself. Poetry is one such example.

Because postmodern thought is nervous of the natural, except when it arrives in the form of rain forests, it tends to overlook the way in which humans are cusped between nature and culture (a cusping of great interest to psychoanalysis), and brusquely reduces them to the latter. Culturalism is quite as much a form of reductionism as biologism or economism, words at the sound of which all stout postmodernists have been trained to make the vampire sign. And the body is the most palpable index of this in-betweenness – more so perhaps than language, which is also an activity of our species being but which seems much more on the side of culture. If soul discourse is to be replaced by body discourse, then one can see the point of dropping talk of *having* a body and substituting talk of *being* one. If my body is something I use or possess on the analogy of a can-opener, then it might be thought that I would have need of another body inside this one to do the using, and so on in an infinite regress. But this resolute anti-dualism, though salutary in some ways, is also untrue to a lot of our intuitions about the lump of flesh we lug around. It makes perfect sense to speak of using my body, as when I suspend it courageously across a crevasse so that my companions can scramble to safety over my spine. We objectify our own bodies and those of others all the time, as a necessary dimension of our being, and postmodernism is quite mistaken to believe, with Hegel rather than Marx, that all objectification is tantamount to alienation. Plenty of objectionable objectification certainly goes on; but the fact remains that human bodies are indeed material objects, and if they were not there could be no question of relationship between them. That the human body is an object is by no means its most distinctive feature, but it is the condition for anything more creative that it can get up to. Unless you can objectify me, there can be no talk of reciprocity between us.

Merleau-Ponty recalls us to the fleshly self, to the situated, incarnate nature of being. His colleague Jean-Paul Sartre has a somewhat less upbeat narrative to tell of the body as that 'outside' of ourselves which we can never quite get a fix on, that unmasterable otherness which threatens to deliver us to the petrifying gaze of the observer. Sartre is anti-Cartesian enough in his idea of human consciousness as mere hankering vacancy, but sufficiently Cartesian in his sense of the nameless gap which separates mind from members. The truth of the body does not lie, as the liberals like to think, somewhere in between, but in the impossible tension between these two versions of bodiliness, both of which are phenomenologically just. It is not quite true that I have a body, and not quite true that I am one either. This deadlock runs all the way through psychoanalysis, which acknowledges that the body is constructed in language, but which knows too that it will never be entirely at home there. For Jacques Lacan, the body articulates itself in signs only to find itself betrayed by them. The transcendental signifier which would say it all, wrap up my demand and deliver it to you whole and entire, is that imposture known as the phallus; and since the phallus does not exist, my bodily desire is doomed to grope its laborious way from partial sign to partial sign, diffusing and fragmenting as it goes.

It is perhaps for this reason that Romanticism has dreamed of the Word of words, of a discourse as firm as flesh, or of a body which had all the universal availability of a language while sacrificing none of its sensuous substance. And there is a sense in which contemporary literary theory, with its excited talk of the materiality of the text, its constant interchanges of the somatic and semiotic, is the latest version of this vision, in suitably disenchanted postmodern style. 'Material' is one of the great buzz-words of such theory, a sound at which all progressive heads reverently bow; but it has now been stretched beyond all feasible sense. For if even meaning is material, then there is nothing which is not, and the term simply cancels all the way through. The new somatics restores us to the creaturely in an abstracted world, and this represents one of its enduring achievements; but in banishing the ghost from the machine, it risks dispelling subjectivity itself as no more than a humanist myth. In doing so, it is in full flight from a liberal humanism whose ideas of the subject are indeed seriously inadequate; and it is to this pitched battle between liberalism and postmodernism that we may now turn.

Nobody is in any doubt about what it is that all men and women want, only about what it means. What everyone wants is happiness, despite Marx and Nietzsche's withering opinion that only the English desired *that*. But this was a smack at the peculiarly anaemic version of happiness espoused by the English Utilitarians, for whom happiness is an essentially unproblematic issue, reducible in effect to pleasure. But to attain happiness I must sometimes pass up on short-term pleasures; and if happiness were not as opaque and bedevilled a notion as it is, we would presumably not have landed ourselves with those convoluted discourses known as moral philosophy, one of whose tasks is to examine what human happiness consists in and how it might be achieved.

The dawning of modernity was the moment when we began to realize that there were many conflicting versions of the good life; that none of these versions could be unimpeachably grounded; and that, strangely enough, we were no longer able to agree on the most fundamental issues in the field. I say 'strangely enough' because one might have thought that we could have agreed on the basics and then diverged on particulars. But though almost everybody agrees that eating people is wrong, at least if they are still alive at the time, we cannot agree on why we agree on this. With the onset of modernity, humanity enters for the first time upon that extraordinary condition, now thoroughly naturalized in our heads, in which we fail to see eye to eye on all the most vital matters – a condition which would have been mind-bendingly unimaginable for some of the ancients, and which seems to forestall all possibility of constructing a life in common.

The political upshot of this condition is liberalism. If there are many different conceptions of the good, then the state must be so constructed as to accommodate them all. The just state is one neutral in respect of any particular conception of the good life, confining its jurisdiction to furnishing the conditions in which individuals may discover it for themselves. It does this by guaranteeing each individual the so-called primary goods necessary for such exploration, while protecting them from being unjustly constrained in this enterprise by the actions of others. There is a contention between libertarian and welfarist liberals about how far this political initiative should extend: should it stretch, as the welfarist believes, to helping to keep people alive, since their pursuit of the good life would otherwise be gravely impeded, or would this itself constitute an undue infringement of their liberty? Whatever this dispute, everyone must receive equal consideration in this respect, for everyone has as much right to the good life as everyone else. But the good life cannot be predefined, partly because there are many different versions of it around, partly because discovering or creating it for oneself may actually be a part of it. For modernity, any good which I have not personally authenticated is rather less good than it could have been.

In a move which much of antiquity would have found astonishing, then, the good life has now become a private affair, while the business of enabling it remains public. For many ancient theorists, no such distinction between the ethical and political was imaginable. The ideology of civic or republican humanism sees each in terms of the other: for me to exercise virtue, to realize my powers and capacities as a self-determining being, just is among other things for me to participate with others in the running of the *polis*. There can be no such thing as private virtue, or a conception of the good life which was mine alone.

The liberal idea of the state, as its more astute apologists acknowledge, is clearly paradoxical. For to claim that the state should be neutral in respect of the good seems inevitably to assert a certain conception of the good, and thus not to be neutral at all. It is also to imply a certain definition of the bad: namely, any individually or collectively pursued 'good' whose consequences would prove inimical to the state's ethical *apatheia*. It belongs to the integrity of the liberal state that it accommodates both socialists and conservatives; but it cannot really look indifferently on their projects, since if realized they might undermine its own indifference. To this extent, one might claim, the liberal state is itself a sort of 'subject', with desires and aversions of its own, even if it understands itself as the mere subjectless preconditions of our subjectivity. Because its very structures inevitably allow for the generating of interests hostile to them, it is not so much neutral as tolerant, and tolerance is a virtue which only subjects can practise.

This point, however, should not be mistaken for the usual reach-me-down leftist case that disinterestedness speciously masks a set of interests. The disinterestedness of the liberal state is *obviously* an interest in itself, and there is no reason why a liberal should be coy about this. My indifference to your moral torment doesn't mask my real attitude to you; it *is* my real attitude to you, and not one I am bothered to dissemble. I am indifferent to your torment because I regard it as in your best interests for me to be so; there have been too many meddling do-gooders around the place already. The interest of the liberal state is to be, within certain stringent limits, genuinely disinterested – not to care what kind of goods people come up with, because it believes that it has no rights in the matter and that this is the morally correct stance to adopt. That disinterestedness is a form of interest may be paradoxical, but it is not necessarily hypocritical or self-contradictory. From a communitarian standpoint, the liberal state is to be chided not because it pretends not to care when it secretly does, but because it really doesn't care and ought to. The communitarian claims that the state ought to concern itself more actively with the definition of the good life; but he or she acknowledges that this state does care a great deal about creating the preconditions for it – cares because it values individual flourishing, and because it passionately believes that disinterestedness, which is to say privileging no one of these individuals in their conception of what counts as such flourishing – is the best way to foster it all round.

In this respect, if not in certain others, liberalism is a paradoxical rather than incoherent doctrine, and some commonplace left criticisms of it thus fall to the ground. So do some of the now boringly familiar protests against its individualism.

Liberalism is indeed a species of individualism, but the left commonly misrecognizes the level at which this is pitched. In a convenient piece of straw-targeting, all liberalism is seen as promoting some primitive Hobbesian notion of the self as a naked natural atom anterior to its social conditions, linked to other such anti-social atoms by a set of purely contractual relations external to its inner substance. It doesn't sound too beguiling, but some postmodernists actually seem to imagine that this is what all liberals must by definition hold. The history of Western philosophy, so we are asked to believe, is by and large the narrative of this starkly autonomous subject, in contrast to the dispersed, divided subject of current postmodern orthodoxy. This ignorant and dogmatic travesty of Western philosophy should not go unchallenged. For Spinoza, the subject is the mere function of an implacable determinism, its 'freedom' no more than the knowledge of iron necessity. The self for David Hume is a convenient fiction, a bundle of ideas and experiences whose unity we can only hypothesize. Kant's moral subject is indeed autonomous and self-determining, but in a mysterious way quite at odds with its empirical determining. For Schelling, Hegel and the other Idealists, the subject is relational to its roots, as it is of course for Marx; for Kierkegaard and Sartre the self is agonizedly non-self-identical, and for Nietzsche mere spume on the wave of the ubiquitous will to power. So much, then, for the grand narrative of the unified subject. That there is indeed such an animal haunting Western thought is not in question; but the tale is far less conveniently homogeneous than some postmodernist devotees of heterogeneity would persuade us to think. There is no need for the liberal tradition to posit some *ontological* individualism. Any reasonably sophisticated liberal can agree that the subject is culturally constructed and historically conditioned; what he or she may be urging is less a philosophical anthropology than a political doctrine concerning that subject's rights in the face of state power. And there is no reason either why such rights should always be conceived in some implausibly naturalistic, Rousseau-like sense. 'Rights' may just refer to those human needs and capacities which are so vital for our thriving and well-being that the state feels constrained to single them out for special protection.

For all that, however, the fact remains that liberalism *is* a kind of individualism, as its political theory attests. What is wrong with the disinterestedness of the liberal state is not that it speciously masks some interest, but that it quite explicitly enshrines one: the all-important interest of individual choice. It is not flawed because it has a notion of the good which it furtively conceals, but because it has a drastically one-sided idea of the good to which other goods are unduly subordinated. And here it really could be accused of bordering upon incoherence. For as Charles Taylor has argued, assigning a right implies that the capacity protected by that right should be positively nurtured; it would be odd to single out some need or capacity in this way and then be blithely indifferent as to whether it flourished or not. But this in turn implies fostering, through our political participation, the kind of social order which would allow this to happen, which might then be taken as challenging the liberal assumption of the primacy of political rights.[1]

We are plunged here in the mighty opposition between deontologists and teleologists, Kantians and Utilitarians, the apologists for the primacy of rights and justice as against the torchbearers for virtue and happiness. Deontological theorists, like Kant or the great contemporary liberal scholar John Rawls, give priority to the right over the good, justice over happiness, whereas teleological moralists like Marxists, Utilitarians and communitarians think that it is happiness or the good life that should lie at the centre of our attention, and that talk of rights is meaningful only within this context. A full-blooded deontologist like Kant holds that actions are right or wrong quite independently of whether they happen to maximize human happiness, whereas a Utilitarian believes, broadly speaking, that right action just is such maximization. For Kant, to ponder the possible beneficial effects of my action is already to have tainted its moral purity; for one rather hard-nosed brand of Utilitarianism, what matters is the promotion of the general well-being even if this means sacrificing the freedom or well-being of particular individuals. All sorts of trade-offs between the two cases are of course possible: most of us would probably agree that there are constraints on what can be demanded of one individual for the common good – that, as Rawls would put it, each person's good matters equally in a way that constrains the pursuit of the good as a whole; but many of us might also find persuasive the teleological claim that moral discourse ought to concern more than just the preconditions of the good life – the equal distribution of freedom, for example – but should also examine in the manner of classical antiquity what the good life might consist in and how best we might secure it. It has been claimed, for example, that Marx is a 'mixed deontologist', who views the moral good as the promotion of general well-being, but not, say, at the expense of the deontological imperative that all men and women have a right to participate in this process.[2]

There is a standard socialist critique of liberalism, which it is worth rehearsing briefly here before passing to some rather less well-thumbed criticisms of the doctrine. This is the case that from one viewpoint liberalism really is self-contradictory, since the very conditions which are meant to secure the good life serve only to undermine it. As long as individual rights centrally include property rights (which is not, it would seem, the case with John Rawls), the liberal state will engender precisely the kinds of inequality and exploitation which subvert the pursuit of the good life it was meant to promote. Everyone will not in fact be in possession of the primary goods necessary to hack their own path to happiness. Some of them will be deprived of the necessary material and spiritual resources, including that esteem of others which is arguably a vital component of human well-being. Since this strikes me as a watertight criticism, I shall not dwell on it here; suffice it to say that Rawls, in his magisterial *A Theory of Justice*, has a single reference to exploitation, and that in a footnote. But a different kind of critique of liberalism has sprung up in recent times from communitarian thinkers like Charles Taylor and Alasdair

MacIntyre – the former a lapsed Catholic, the latter, in an agreeable symmetry, a recent convert. This position, in MacIntyre's case an intriguing *mélange* of Aristotle, Aquinas and Wittgenstein, attends to the cultural and historical roots of the self, its embodiment in tradition and community, and from this vantage-point upbraids what it sees as the abstract Enlightenment atomism of the liberal subject, with its ahistorical, speciously universalist ethics.[3]

I have suggested already that there is no reason for the canny liberal to deny the culturalist case. But there is no reason either why she should deny the value of community, since this is clearly one good which many individuals seek and which the liberal state must therefore accommodate. As far as the liberal is concerned, men and women are perfectly free to pursue communitarian ends, if this happens to be the form of the good life they choose; it is just that such communitarianism must not be *built into* the state, since this might constitute an undue infringement of the rights of those who wished to pursue happiness by sitting in a darkened room with a paper bag over their head. One might argue that if political arrangements are of the socialist, civic humanist, communitarian or Habermasian sort which demands that I spend a good deal of time in community activities or collective decision-making, then I have less time to pass the whole of my waking life trying on one leather costume after another in the privacy of my bedroom; and if this happens to constitute the good life for me, then it behoves the state not to discriminate against me in this flagrantly prejudicial manner.

The state itself, in short, must not rank goods hierarchically; but from a socialist point of view it has already done so. For it has ruled out forms of community at the level of its own structures, and thus, for example, censored any move to bring economic life into more cooperative control. Such an arrangement would no doubt interfere with rival conceptions of the good which the liberal state must also permit to thrive. The state itself is not in the business of adjudicating between alternative notions of happiness. It has no more view than a giraffe has on the question of whether bouncing around in a leather apron is more or less valuable than the democratic management of the economy. Its only concern is that no specific conception of the good life should be built into its own structures. But since the socialist management of the economy would be impossible without such a project, it has succeeded in ruling it out while appearing to preserve a neutral stance towards it. The liberal state does not rule out socialism because it considers it to lack value, since it has no opinion on the matter. It excludes it for the reasons I have mentioned, which would mean having itself to privilege a particular ideology. But the grounds on which it refuses to do this are arguably themselves ideological: the sovereignty of individual choice.

If the liberal state is fearful that socialism would limit the plurality of goods available to individuals. I think this fear can be shown to be baseless. First of all, socialism, which like widespread virtue is only feasible if you are reasonably well-heeled as a society,[4] would considerably augment the primary goods available to each individual for her pursuit of happiness, by seeking to eliminate want. Moreover, not only would it construct the institutions of community without any necessary detriment to other, more personally selected goods; it would actually expand that area of personal choice, by (for example) shortening the working day and so increasing leisure time. One of the best reasons for being a socialist is that one is averse to doing too much work. In this sense, more communal social structures, and a plurality of personal goods, are not for socialism ultimately antithetical, and the conflict between communitarian and liberal is to this extent resolved. One can put this case in other terms too. The liberal objects to socialism, among other reasons, because he fears that everyone would end up believing the same thing, sharing the same notion of the good life, and so fatally impoverishing freedom of individual action and the plurality of possible goods. The communitarian objects to liberalism exactly because in liberal society men and women *don't* share common life-forms on any pervasive scale, and are thus rootless, atomized, disinherited. Socialism, however, combines the best of liberalism and communitarianism in this sense too. It shares with the latter a belief in the collective determination of meanings and values, as well as in the cultural and historical shapings of the self; but it holds that this collective determination will result in the sort of heterogeneous social order the liberal most admires, rather than in the potentially autocratic, sheep-like set of communities to which some communitarian theory ominously points. In practice, such theory sometimes seems to mean that if you smoke on the street or commit adultery in certain towns, your neighbours land collectively on your doorstep and beat you up.

The fact that the collective shaping of values would mean more rather than less plurality is only not seen because of a crucial ambiguity in the phrase 'common culture'. A common culture can mean one commonly shared, or one commonly fashioned; and if communitarians consider that the latter necessarily implies the former, then they are surely mistaken. For the fact is that if everyone is able to participate fully in the moulding of that culture, through the institutions of socialist democracy, the upshot is likely to be a culture far more heterogeneous than one bound together by a shared 'world view'. This, presumably, is what Raymond Williams has in mind when he writes that 'A common culture is not, at any level, an equal culture . . . A culture in common, in our own day, will not be the simple all-in-all society of old dream. It will be a very complex organization, requiring continual adjustment and redrawing . . . We have to ensure the means of life, and the means of community. But what will then, by these means, be lived, we cannot know or say'.[5] We would expect a common culture to share certain values simply by virtue of its commonness: a commitment, for example, to the sustaining of what Williams calls 'the means of community'. But if the culture were common in the sense of engaging the active participation of all its members, then we would equally expect it to produce a plurality of values and life-forms. For the socialist, as for the republican humanist,[6] the process of sharing in political life is itself a matter of virtue, a vital means by which one exercises

common with communitarianism – embarrassing, because neither Richard Rorty nor Alasdair MacIntyre would be much complimented by being told that they were in some respects mirror-images. Like communitarianism, postmodernism can generally find little but error in the Enlightenment; it also highlights the cultural and historical fashioning of the self to the point where to submit those forces to radical critique would involve, as we have seen, some leap into metaphysical outer space. Communitarianism has a similar problem, to say the least, with how its communal norms or traditions would be subject to critical self-monitoring. Both creeds are brands of culturalism, maintaining that right action or the good life cannot be defined apart from the contingent cultural practices we have inherited. The self for both doctrines is embedded in a purely parochial history, and moral judgements thus cannot be universal. Moral judgements, for Rorty and his ilk, really say 'We don't do that kind of thing around here'; whereas for a woman to say 'sexual discrimination is wrong' usually means that we *do* do that kind of thing around here but we shouldn't.[7] The case, anyway, begins to fray at the edges a little when you realize that people do many conflicting things within the same culture, and are quite often heirs to several irreconcilable traditions. Conventionalism or communitarianism needs to keep its forms of life fairly unitary, with no grievous internal divisions. There are, of course, key differences between the two currents: the bourgeois liberalism which Rorty frankly endorses has nothing much in common with MacIntyre's neo-Aristotelianism, and the former is prepared to be a good deal more ironic about his allegiances than the latter. But for both viewpoints, the self is at its best when it belongs to a set of local cultural practices, however hybridized those may be for the postmodernists and homogeneous for the communitarians.

At its least appealing, then, postmodernism presses the communitarian standpoint towards a lopsided culturalism, moral relativism and hostility to universals, in contrast to a socialism which shares with that standpoint its more positive values of community, historicity and relationality. But postmodern theory then proceeds to combine all this with some of the least palatable aspects of the very liberalism which the communitarians view as their enemy. It has little to say of the great liberal motifs of justice, freedom, equality, human rights and the like, since these topics sit uncomfortably with its nervousness of the 'autonomous subject'. And since it is wary for similar reasons of the ancient or positive conception of liberty as self-determination, it is forced to fall back on the modern or negative notion of liberty as doing your own thing free of external constraint. We have seen already, however, that it presses this freedom to the point where the subject risks imploding upon itself, leaving nothing much to experience the freedom in question. The classical liberal subject at least strived to preserve its identity and autonomy along with its plurality, though this was never an easy matter; now, in a drastic declension of that process, the subject of a more advanced phase of middle-class society is compelled to sacrifice its truth and identity to its plurality, to which it then mystifyingly gives the name of freedom. Or, to put the point another way, the strenuously productive self of liberal capitalism is yielding ground to the consumerist subject of a later stage of that same history.

The freedom of the classical liberal subject was always curbed, in theory at least, by its respect for the autonomy of others. Without such respect it would risk collapse, since others would then not respect its autonomy either. But if there are no autonomous others out there, then the freedom of the subject, in fantasy at least, comes bursting through the juridico-political frame which once contained it. This, however, is something of a Pyrrhic victory, since there is also no longer any unified subject in here to whom the liberty in question might be attached. If that liberty involves the dissolution of the unified subject, then it can logically be no freedom at all. All the subject would seem to be free of is itself. We have arrived at a libertarianism without a subject, which suggests that what was standing in the way of the subject's freedom was nothing less than the subject itself. And this is an appropriate enough image of existing society, in which for

Marx the limit of capital is capital itself, and which presents itself as a continually self-thwarting culture. The autonomous subject of this social order is at once the source of freedom and, in the shape of both itself and its competitors, the obstacle to it.

One could imagine, then, such a subject dreaming of dismantling these inconveniently autonomous others, even if the price of that victory would be the simultaneous dissolution of the self which confronts them. Or, to put it another way, everyone has now been converted into consumers, mere empty receptacles of desire. In place of those old autonomous others, who were all too stubbornly specific, there now emerges a portentously generalized Otherness, the particular bearers of which can become indifferently interchangeable: women, Jews, prisoners, gays, aboriginal peoples. Such abstracting is hardly in the spirit of postmodern particularism; nor is it all that complimentary to inform these 'others' that they are just some generalized signifier of Otherness, for which purpose any bunch of them would presumably do just as well as any other. Otherness in this sense is by no means the opposite of exchange-value. What homogenizes these avatars of Otherness is just the fact that none of them is me, or us, which implies quite as self-centred a perspective as the most discreditable 'humanist' subject. If the 'other' is reduced to whatever disrupts my identity, is this a humbly decentring move, or a self-regarding one? And if the world is hollowed out along with me, as a fractured subject confronts a fictional reality, is that subject really as humble as it seems if it has made sure that there is no longer any obdurate reality out there to resist it?

We have seen already that the postmodern subject is in some paradoxical sense both 'free' and determined, 'free' *because* constituted to its core by a diffuse set of forces. In this sense it is at once more and less free than the autonomous subject which preceded it. On the one hand, the culturalist bias of postmodernism can push towards a full-blooded determinism: we just are ineluctably shaped by power or desire or conventions or interpretative communities into particular behaviours and beliefs. You do not avoid the demeaning implications of this with the escape clause of *over*determination – that the systems which compose us are after all multiple and conflicting rather than monolithic, thus lending the subject a lack of fixed identity which it can come to mistake for its freedom. An electron has no fixed positionality either, but we do not congratulate it on its emancipated condition. Like all such social determinism, this viewpoint is offensive to the rational dignity of human beings, whose rationality may well be a good deal frailer than most rationalists seem to think, but who are not thereby to be reduced to some brainy sort of trout.

What is omitted from this picture is the fact that human beings are determined precisely in a way which allows them a degree of self-determination, and that any final opposition between the conditioned and the autonomous is consequently false. That we are, within reasonable limits, self-determining is not because we are grandly autonomous of our environment but exactly because such self-determination is a necessity of it. If we were not able to be tolerably self-motivating we would almost certainly not be around to tell the tale, which would be a death of the subject of a rather different kind. Just to survive, the human animal cannot rely on instinct but must bring self-reflective resources into play. To register the patronizing quality of this cultural determinism, one has only to ask oneself whether it would be so readily asserted of, say, African Americans or the Liverpool Irish that they were the mere prisoners of their unthinking conventions, tribalist in the most pejorative sense of the term. Yet something like this is sometimes claimed of, say, American academia, where one can get away with calling them a code-bound tribe because it seems an iconoclastic deflation of Western rationalist pretensions, and so anti-ethnocentric rather than objectionable.

If the postmodern subject is determined, however, it is also strangely free-floating, contingent, aleatory, and so a kind of caricatured version of the negative liberty of the liberal self. We have seen already how it is the concept of heterogeneity which pins these antithetical ideas together: if this subject is slippery, it is because it acts as the friction between clashing cultural forces. There is much of the Nietzschean will to power in this vision; but it also corresponds pretty well to the experience of advanced capitalist societies. (I avoid the term 'late', since we have no idea just how late they are.) Where else do you feel at once moulded by implacably determining forces and alarmingly adrift? This subject is in some ways as much a creature of the marketplace as was the very different subject of classical liberalism, which also, incidentally, had a problem in reconciling its freedom with its determinism. Kant's duality of noumenal and phenomenal selves is in this sense no more than a confession of defeat. But as long as some sort of autonomous subject seemed to survive, however unaccountably, it was at least possible to speak of justice. If there are no such subjects around, then all the vital questions over which classical political philosophy has agonized – your rights against mine, my struggle for emancipation against yours – can simply be dissolved away.

Nobody, of course, believes this for a moment. Even postmodernists are worthy of justice and esteem: even they are in this reasonable sense of the phrase autonomous subjects, as they might recognize if only they could relinquish a shoddy caricature of the notion which has been credited by fewer thinkers than they imagine. It is tiresomely dogmatic to maintain that autonomous, self-determining subjects must inevitably be seamless, atomistic, non-relational, dehistoricized, metaphysically grounded and the rest – a lot of self-righteous banging at a door which was never quite so tightly shut. There are indeed such virulent ideologies around, and postmodernism has done some sterling work in its efforts to dislodge them. If it is true that its sense of the subject can sail perilously close to naturalizing consumerism, it is also true that this shattered, schizoid, emptily yearning self bears more than a passing resemblance to the condition of the dispossessed. The famous decentred subject has indeed proved something of a scandal to those rather too full of themselves. It has also helped to deflate a political left which thought that the point was simply to act rather than to problematize the nature of the agent, which is to say themselves. It has spoken to the situation of the gagged and anonymous, and its ability to discern power in powerlessness, to divine the formidable force of *kenosis*, has behind it a precious spiritual tradition which knows how to conjure force out of failure. This is a paradox which can figure only as folly to the prevailing powers, which is the exact measure of its wisdom.

There is indeed, then, a genuine as well as bogus form of otherness, and postmodern thought at its most creative has been able to tap something of its elusive power. If we were really able to divest ourselves of the centred ego, rather than merely enjoy the act of theorizing about it, then there is surely no doubt that a great power for political good would be unleashed. But we are trapped in this respect between two epochs, the one dying and the other powerless to be born. The old 'liberal humanist' self, which chalked up some remarkable achievements in its time, was able to transform the world, but only at the price of a self-violence which at times made it seem hardly worth the cost. The deconstructed self which followed on its heels has still to demonstrate that the non-identical can transform as well as subvert, and the omens so far have not been auspicious. There remains, however, one model which promises to bring identity and decentrement into fruitful alliance, a model which returns us to the themes we have outlined above. The idea of socialist democracy would seem to involve at once self-determination and self-decentring, as the freely self-fashioning subject, precisely because it is not alone in its project, is at the same time always non-self-identical, extrinsic to itself in some complex reciprocity, receiving back its desire from the place of the Other. In this sense, at least, the stalely familiar opposition between 'humanist' and 'decentred' subjects is quite misleading, since to be decentred in one sense of the term, constituted through and through by otherness, belongs to our human natures. It is by restoring this social dimension of subjectivity that we can avoid both the humanist mistake of simply modelling political solidarity along the lines of a singular self-determining subject, now suitably collectivized but otherwise largely unaltered, and the myopia of a subject which suspects solidarity itself as some oppressively normalizing consensus.

There are limits, however, to any such merely theoretical 'resolution'. If we cannot yet provide any less abstract response to the problem, it is not because we lack the intelligence, but because, as with most recalcitrant theoretical questions, we find ourselves here running our heads up against the current limits of language – which is of course to say the current limits of our political world.

5
Fallacies

Speaking as a hierarchical, essentialistic, teleological, metahistorical, universalist humanist, I imagine I have some explaining to do. What I mean, I suppose, is that one could surely find meanings for all of those terms which were more radical than the current post-modern canards would have it. Let us take the easier ones first.

It is a mistake to confuse hierarchy with elitism. The term 'elite' is itself nebulous enough, and is sometimes conflated with 'vanguard', which (whether one approves of vanguards or not) is quite a different matter. Elitism is a belief in the authority of a select few, which in cultural terms usually suggests that values either are or should be the preserve of a privileged group, self-elected or otherwise, one which derives its authority either from some status other than its cultural standing (its social or religious background, for example), or from its cultural clout alone. Such elitism is not at all incompatible with a certain vein of populism, as the thought of W. B. Yeats, T. S. Eliot and Benito Mussolini amply demonstrates. It may be that the *definition* of values is monopolized by this coterie, but that these values are then disseminated by it downwards, to end up in the popular consciousness either self-intact or suitably modified. All the most effective forms of elitism are also populist to their core. 'Hierarchy', a term which originally denoted the three categories of angels, has come to mean any kind of gradated structure, not necessarily a social one. In its broadest sense, it refers to something like an order of priorities.

In this broad sense of the word, everyone is a hierarchist, whereas not everyone is an elitist. Indeed you may object to elites because they offend your order of priorities. Democracy is not the absence of ranking: on the contrary, it involves privileging the interests of the people as a whole over the interests of anti-social power-groups. Everyone subscribes to some hierarchy of values, a commitment which is arguably constitutive of the self. As Charles Taylor puts it: 'To know who you are is to be oriented in moral space, a space in which questions arise about what is good or bad, what is worth doing and what not, what has meaning and importance for you and what is trivial and secondary'.[1] Valuing belongs with social identity, and social life would grind to a halt without it. A subject which really didn't discriminate would not be a human subject at all, which is perhaps why some postmodern subjects who view valuing as 'elitist' can exist only on paper. It is also hard to know from where they derive the value judgement that value is an irrelevance. Cultural theorists sometimes like to feign that value is unimportant, and there was certainly an almighty fetishizing of it in the old-style literary academy; but while the popular-minded intelligentsia deny that George Eliot is superior to *Beavis and Butthead*, the stubbornly evaluative populace continue to prefer one television programme to another.

What is under postmodern fire, however, is perhaps less the notion of some practical ranking of priorities than the assumption that such priorities are eternal and immutable. Conjunctural or provisional priorities are all very well, priorities for certain purposes within certain contexts; it is just *absolute* hierarchies which postmodernists find insidious. But there seems nothing terribly objectionable about absolute hierarchies either. It is hard to imagine a situation in which tickling the starving would be preferable to feeding them, or torturing people less reprehensible than teasing them. Radical politics is necessarily hierarchical in outlook, needing some way of calculating the most effective distribution of its limited energies over a range of issues. It assumes, as does any rational subject, that some issues are more important than others, that some places are preferable starting-points to other places, that some struggles are central to a particular form of life and some are not. It may, of course, disastrously miscalculate such matters, sidelining for decades or even a century or so conflicts which are in fact vital but which it has culpably overlooked. The Marxist left has done precisely this for much of its career. But this is no argument against the fact that some issues are indeed more central than others, a proposition which nobody could conceivably deny because nobody is in this sense of the term a relativist. Those who have been pushed to the margin are not demanding an abandonment of all priorities but a transformation of them. All human practices, from storming the Bastille to brushing one's teeth, work by exclusion, negation, suppression; it is just that one should try to avoid excluding the wrong things or suppressing the wrong people. To argue that one should study *Dallas* rather than *Little Dorrit* is not a levelling of values but a reordering of them. To claim that one should study them both is not a collapsing of values but a different kind of valuation.

Once, however, the possibility of any very ambitious political project has been closed down, it is easy to find the question of priorities irrelevant, since if substantial change is not anyway on the agenda, the business of where to start and how to calculate your energies is neither here nor there. Some radicals might then begin to feel slightly squeamish about the self-evident truth that some issues or artefacts are more precious than others, and mistake this for 'elitism'. This is in fact a category mistake, confusing a social ranking with a theoretical or political one, but it is doubtful if this would be enough to give its exponents pause. They would have failed to realize that social elites and political priorities are not only not analogous, but from a radical viewpoint actually antithetical, since it is one priority of radical politics to challenge the power of social elites. Their 'anti-elitism' would thus play its modest part in keeping such elites in business. They might also fail to notice that the most formidably anti-elitist force in modern capitalist societies is known as the marketplace, which levels all distinctions, garbles all gradations and buries all distinctions of use-value beneath the abstract equality of exchange-value. Such radicals would no doubt be enthusiasts of difference but not of value judgements, which is to say that their attitude towards difference would be perfectly indifferent. But though they might heroically strive to value no particular difference more than another, they would surely come to notice after a while that they were valuing difference as such, and so transgressing their own self-denying ordinance.

There is another potential contradiction to be noted here. Some postmodernists like to make statements like 'Milton isn't better than Superwoman, just different'. And they have certainly done valuable work, if they would allow the adjective, in retrieving whole reaches of previously discarded culture and demonstrating just what a chancy affair the cultural canon is. But it is also typical of some postmodernism to underline just how much our judgements, like everything else about us, are conditioned by our culture. Given a certain aesthetic formation, we just couldn't help seeing Milton as great art, any more than we can help seeing a dingo as a dingo or associating the four black marks 'door' with a piece of wood in the wall. One might pause here to note that value judgements which we can't help making are actually a lot less valuable than those that we can. I am not particularly flattered by your high opinion of me if I know that you are pathologically incapable of saying a bad word about anyone. If I know that you are somehow in a position to make a negative judgement, then the fact that you deliver a positive one commands all the more authority. The point, however, is that there is a tension between this strong cultural determinism on the one hand, and a belief in the revaluation of values on the other. It need not be an outright contradiction: it may be that my subculture has conditioned me to see Mickey Mouse comics as the finest thing since the dizzy heights of *The Boy's Own Weekly*, whereas your dominant culture makes it impossible for you not to regard Milton as magnificent. Short of such situations, however, you cannot really run together a strong culturalism and an audacious reversal of values, since the latter implies a kind of voluntarism which the former denies.

The belief that values are constructed, historically variable and inherently revisable has much to recommend it, though it fares rather better with Gorky than it does with genocide. It sees itself as a counter-Enlightenment move, which in one evident sense it is: values are no longer universal but local, no longer absolute but contingent. In another sense, however, it is merely a reprise of Enlightenment thought. It assumes, just like Enlightenment materialism, a sharp dichotomy between value and fact: the world itself is so much brute, inert, meaningless matter, and value is an imposition upon it. There are no significant hierarchies *in* reality, no sense in which it is the *case* that, say, reducing others to objects of voyeuristic gratification is worse than tending their wounds. As with Kant, the realm of value is one thing and the sphere of nature quite another; the Aristotelian notion that the latter may guide the former is for Kant offensive to the dignity of the self-directing subject, and for postmodernism an objectivist myth. It is ironic that the postmodern scepticism of objective values should land it right back, at one level at least, in the camp of a Reason it seeks to deconstruct.

We may turn next to essentialism, one of the most heinous crimes in the postmodernist book, a well-nigh capital offence or the equivalent in Christian theology to sins against the Holy Spirit. Essentialism in its more innocuous form is the doctrine that things are made up of certain properties, and that some of these properties are actually constitutive of them, such that if they were to be removed or radically transformed the thing in question would then become some other thing, or nothing at all. Stated as such, the doctrine of essentialism is trivially, self-evidently true, and it is hard to see why anyone would want to deny it. It has, as it stands, no very direct political implications, good or bad. Since postmodernists are keen on sensuous particularity, it is surprising in a way that they are so nervous of this belief in the specific whatness of something. There is a harder-nosed version of the doctrine, which holds that there are 'core properties, or clusters of properties, present, necessarily, in all and only those things which bear the common name'.[2] This is clearly much harder to swallow. Some philosophers would doubt that these properties were 'necessary', or that all of them needed to be present in an object of a certain class, or that they all had to be unique to objects of that class. But not many philosophers would doubt that there are certain properties which make a thing what it is, or that things which are members of the same class must have *something* in common, even if that something is no more than a network of 'family resemblances'.

To believe in essentialism is not necessarily to entertain the implausible view that *all* of the properties of a thing are essential to it. Having a certain weight is essential to being human, as having bushy eyebrows is not. Nor is it to assume that there are always sharp breaks between one thing and another, that everything is locked off from everything else in its own watertight ontological space. In fact you may hold with Hegel and others that the relationality of things is precisely of their essence. For something to display certain essential properties does not necessarily mean that we always know for sure where it ends and another object begins. A field with uncertain boundaries can still be a field, and the indeterminacy of its frontiers does not throw everything within them into ontological turmoil. People might once have been in doubt about whether Strasburg was a French or a German possession, but this does not mean that they were in doubt about which Berlin was. There is no reason either to assume that for things to belong to the same class means that they all display exactly the same essential features, with certain minor variants which make of them different objects. We do not call a lot of very different kinds of writing 'literary criticism' because they all share exactly the same general features, and some of these features they will share with writing which we don't call literary criticism. But to call both Joseph Addison and William Empsom literary critics is to claim that they have *certain* properties in common, even if we turn out to be wrong about this.

Nor does a belief in essentialism necessarily commit one to the view that there is only ever *one*, central property which makes a thing what it is. Essentialism is not necessarily a form of reductionism. It need not involve believing that there is never any doubt about what is essential to something and what is not. On the contrary, it can be the subject of infinite debate. Some people hold that the monarchy is essential to Britain's being what it is, while other people take leave to doubt this fantasy. All kinds of liminal cases are possible, such as wondering whether a bicycle with no wheels, seat or handlebars is still a bicycle, or whether a boat which you have completely rebuilt plank by plank over a period of time is still the boat you began with. What is and isn't essential to being human may be relevant to debates about abortion, or for that matter to imperialism: you might feel happier about slaughtering the natives if you considered that they lacked some property or properties which you took to be definitive of being human. If there is indeed such a thing as human nature, we might very well never come to agree on what it essentially consists in, as the philosophical record to date would strongly intimate.

I have said that transforming or removing some essential property of something would mean that it changed its nature, but one might think this should be qualified when we come to social phenomena. It is hard to see how water which wasn't wet would still be water, but one could always argue that what is taken to be essential about human beings and their institutions is historically variable. Some cultures have thought that it is of the essence of being female that you should be subjugated, whereas others have not, or at least not officially. You could have, in other words, a kind of historically relativized essentialism, believing for instance that being courageous was necessarily part of being a warrior in the ancient sagas, whereas being brave is not necessarily part of what it means to be a soldier today. A cowardly officer is still for us an officer, at least until he is cashiered, whereas a cowardly leader for certain premodern societies would have been no kind of leader at all. For them, certain virtues were essential to performing certain social roles, which is not always true of us today.

One should beware, however, of pushing this relativism too far. Those cultures which have held that women have some qualities simply as women which make them eminently oppressible are wrong. Whether they are wrong because women have in fact no determinate nature at all, either oppressible or non-oppressible, or because women have a right not to be oppressed just as a consequence of being human, is a matter for debate between postmodernists and some of their critics. To say that women should never be oppressed anywhere just on account of their common humanity sounds like a more forceful criticism of patriarchy than to say that they have no common humanity to begin with, but many postmodernists fear that one would pay for this strong ethical defence by essentializing women in the manner of some of their subjugators. I say *some* of their subjugators, since there is of course no necessity for oppressors to be essentialist either. It is perfectly possible, in theory at least, for them to be full-blooded culturalists, who defend their predatory behaviour on purely conventionalist grounds. In fact this is more likely to be true of some hard-boiled business executives today than it would have been of Cardinal Wolsey. The ancient Greek Sophists were conventionalists, but they were not notable for their attempts to emancipate ancient Greek slaves. Indeed if all cultural conventions are equally arbitrary, why not just commit yourself, as the Sophists did, to the set you find yourself inhabiting, even if it happens to include sexism?

Essentialism, then, is not necessarily a characteristic of the political right, or anti-essentialism an indispensable feature of the left. Karl Marx was an essentialist,[3] whereas Jeremy Bentham, father of bourgeois Utilitarianism, was a zealous anti-essentialist. John Locke, father of English liberalism and investor in the slave trade, believed that some essences were real, but others merely 'nominal'. As Denys Turner has written:

> No attribute ... is [for Locke] any more essentially a constituent of reality than any other. From this it follows that there is also no reason why one should not regard any particular attribute one chooses as being essential ... if no characteristic essentially defines a human person, then there is no reason why skin-colour should be taken as doing so. Equally, and this is the permission granted to the racist, if any characteristic might just as well be an essential characteristic of the human person, there is no reason why skin-colour should not be made to be so. Generally, if every difference in point of fact is equally a matter of indifference in point of morals, it is never possible to show why I should not take any difference I choose as making in point of morals *all* the difference.[4]

Like postmodernism, Locke throws out human essences and believes that what matters about human beings is just a question of what we construct as mattering. It is just that postmoderns are anti-racist anti-essentialists, whereas he is a racist anti-essentialist. Neither party can accuse the other of being wrong in point of fact. The radical essentialist (or moral realist) case against them both is that it is a fact that skin colour is not definitive of human beings, in the sense that to be black is not to be of a different species from those who are white. Death is essential to human beings, but freckles are not. What culture you inhabit is not definitive of your humanity, in the sense that beings of different cultures are not creatures of different species. To be *some* kind of cultural being is indeed essential to our humanity, but not to be any particular kind. There are no non-cultural human beings, not because culture is all there is to human beings, but because culture belongs to their nature. Human nature is always incarnate in some specific cultural mode, just as all languages are specific. It is this that one sort of liberal humanist overlooks, in imagining that there is a central core of immutable values beneath the relative trivia of our cultural differences. Where the culturalist goes wrong, by contrast, is to think that because all languages are specific they cannot be spoken of as *language* at all. This makes it hard to see exactly *what* is being proposed here as culturally specific. If claiming that all languages are specific means that there is no such general thing as language, how do we come to identify that the activity whose specificity we are urging is language in the first place, rather than, say, playing badminton or blowing your nose? Postmodern culturalism is a form of philosophical nominalism, which teaches that general categories are unreal, and so has much in common with the Lockean empiricism it professes to scorn. The fact that postmodernists have learnt to be good anti-empiricists occasionally just means that they display a prejudice against what the rest of us call facts. 'Positivism' and 'empiricism', two quite different philosophical currents, can then be used interchangeably to rebuke anyone who mentions that Shakespeare's birthday fell in April.

One can put the case for essentialism in a negative form. Words like 'feminism' and 'socialism' are unwieldly, portmanteau categories which cover a complex range of beliefs and activities and accommodate an immense amount of disagreement. There is no question of their being tightly bounded or impermeable, any more than the rest of our language is. It is precisely because language is rough-hewn stuff rather than glacially smooth that it works so well. A 'perfect' language would be quite useless for social existence. It is possible these days to find people who reject the labour theory of value, the idea of false consciousness, the model of base and superstructure, the notion of political revolution, the tenets of dialectical materialism, the doctrine of the conflict between the forces and relations of production, the law of the falling rate of profits and the project of abolishing market relations and commodity production. Yet these people still insist on calling themselves Marxists. They mean by this, one presumes, that they consider none of these teachings as belonging to the essence of Marxism. There were neo-Kantian Marxists a century or so ago who suspected that although socialism was inevitable, it was by no means necessarily desirable. If, however, they had clamoured at the same time for a speedy return to feudalism, it might have been rather less confusing for them to have called themselves something else. It is also possible to stumble across devout Christians who do not believe in God. Does this then mean that terms like 'Marxist' and 'Christian' can mean just anything? Surely not: any term which tried to cover everything would end up meaning nothing in particular, since signs work by virtue of their differences. This is one reason why not everything can be material, or political, or ideological, as some incautious radicals seem to think. If we encountered someone who called herself a feminist while forcing as many women as she could into sweated labour, then we would conclude that she was not in fact a feminist even though she thought she was. We would not take her at her word, however much she might piously proclaim the validity of her own experience. Someone who avowed his passion for pork sausages but almost never ate them and betrayed all the signs of profound revulsion when he did would presumably be either mad, mendacious, deeply self-deceived or just incompetent in handling the phrase 'a passion for'. If terms like 'feminist' and 'socialist' are to retain their force, there must be something with which they are incompatible. There must be something, not necessarily one thing, which for the moment at least counts as being a feminist rather than a non-feminist; and it is just this that the milder versions of the much-maligned concept of essentialism are trying to get at. Postmodernism is against essentialism; but it is also against metanarratives, universal Reason and non-pluralist cultures, and these views are arguably essential to it.

For all that, of course, postmodern anti-essentialism has a point. There are indeed reductive, falsely eternalizing, brutally homogenizing uses of the concept of essence, and they have wreaked especial havoc in the fields of gender and ethnicity. Essentialism there means something like 'reifying to an immutable nature or type', and has been a potent weapon in the arsenal of the patriarchs, racists and imperialists, even if it has also been brandished by some feminists and ethnic activists themselves. But if every concept which can be used for radical ends was discarded because it can also be deployed against them, the discourse of radicalism would be threadbare indeed. Radicals, for example, should not cease to be traditionalists just because 'tradition' for some other people means the Changing of the Guard rather than the suffragettes. In any case, even though the immutability of a 'bad' essentialism may be politically dangerous in these particular fields, there is no reason to assume dogmatically that the idea of immutability is always so. One would hope that political emancipation would prove immutable, in the sense that it could never be undone. Anyway, on a classical understanding of essence, change is of its essence. We do not react with cries of alarm or shouts of astonishment when a kitten grows into a cat; it is of its nature to do so. We cannot jettison essentialism because we need to know among other things which needs are essential to humanity and which are not. Needs which are essential to our survival and well-being, such as being fed, keeping warm, enjoying the company of others and a degree of physical integrity, can then become politically criterial: any social order which denies such needs can be challenged on the grounds that it is denying our humanity, which is usually a stronger argument against it than the case that it is flouting our contingent cultural conventions. If essentialism is politically important, it is ultimately because radicals confront a formidably powerful system and so stand in need of the most convincing arguments they can muster. If arguments from a common human nature can be deployed to defend the status quo, they can also, in principle at least, have a deeper critical impact upon it than the language of culturalism.

I have suggested already that the brand of teleology postmodernists are most given to admonishing is something of a straw target. Hardly anybody believes that history is smoothly unfurling towards some predetermined goal. But everyone believes in historical purposes and intentions, of projects defined and directed by their particular ends. And most people other than a few seriously bizarre post-structuralists accept the notion of necessary conditions: the banal proposition that there are times when, in order to accomplish *Y*, you must first of all have achieved *X*. If this is obviously true for individuals, it is also true for history in general. And this is at least one fairly minimal sense in which history is a matter of necessity rather than an 'anything goes'. This is not, needless to say, some *built-in* necessity; it is rather the way in which our own free actions are all the time stealthily weaving a tight web of determinations in which we then find ourselves entangled, discovering to our dismay that we have managed to shrink to a few meagre options what previously looked like some infinitely open horizon of possibility. Indeed we are closing down our historical options all the time, simply by opening others up. What looks like the action of some malevolent historical will in the fiction of Thomas Hardy quite often turns out to be just this kind of ironic process, by which our own tolerably free actions in the past now confront us in the present with all the enigmatic opaqueness of some metaphysical destiny.

There is no question, then, of some simple-minded choice between history as story-shaped and history as colourful chaos, of the kind some postmodernists would urge upon us. If narratives are what we live as well as recount, there can be no question of seeing material history as sheer undecidable text, awaiting the artful orderings of some theorist's randomly selected tale. This is the privileged view of those lucky enough not to know that historical projects sometimes have all too determinate goals from the standpoint of their victims. The fact that there is no 'anything goes' for those victims is usually a matter to rue. To deny that history is 'rational' in the sanguine, Hegelian sense of the word is not necessarily to deny that it comes to us in a grimly specific shape. Indeed for Marx history was at once determinate and *ir*rational, and the intention of socialism is to make it rather less of both. Historical indeterminacy, in the sense of a society more laid-back and unconstrained, less in thrall to abstract categories or to forces which knock us sideways like some natural catastrophe, is for socialism a goal still to be achieved, and one which would mean getting out from under the dreary determinacy of the past. A history which was rather more under rational control would loom up a good deal less for us like some implacable fate, which is why, *pace* the postmodernists, it is rationality and freedom which go together. For postmodernism, these things are usually to be found lined up on opposite sides of the theoretical barricades, as an imperious Reason threatens to repel our transgressive desires. In this sense, as we have seen, the postmodern conception of freedom finds it hard to advance very far beyond a negative or old-fashioned liberal one, and at times falls back even from that. But there can be no positive freedom without constraints, since no secure field in which to realize it. It is just that freedom grasped as collective self-determination would also diminish the kinds of constraint which men and women now experience as a kind of second nature, and which confront them with all the sublime authority of some Hardyesque President of the Immortals. And it is Marxism which is supposed to subscribe to some mythological, self-propelling Dialectic of History quite independent of the human will!

If history is fundamentally random, in the sense, for example, that there are no significant causal relations between one bit of it and another, it is difficult to know how one could avoid, say, Stalinism. This may not be the most burning political question for us at the moment, since the (post-)Stalinist societies have just collapsed; but it may serve as an example of a good rather than bad kind of teleological thought. Authoritarian post-capitalist societies are among other things the result of trying to build socialism in dismally unpropitious conditions, without the benefit of developed productive forces, well-heeled allies, non-hostile neighbours, cooperative peasants, a vigorous liberal-democratic tradition, a civil society in good working order, a reasonably well-educated working class and the like. These are necessary if not sufficient conditions for the construction of socialism: there is an important difference between claiming that socialism somehow follows on automatically from capitalism, which really would be a flamboyant bit of teleology, and arguing that a developed capitalism provides some of the necessary conditions for the building of socialism. To embark on the enterprise without them would be to risk ending up with an autocratic state which, in the absence of a middle-class industrial heritage, had to force through the development of industry itself. Someone who regarded all this as 'teleology' in the pejorative sense, with its benightedly 'linear' perspective[5] and trust to 'metaphysical' causality, would be well advised not to take such a dim view of necessary conditions when it came to crossing the high street.

The oldest teleological tales of all tend to run in threes. First we have a golden age of 'primitive' community, blissful but somewhat tedious; then a Fall from this state into an inspiring but disintegrative individualism, and finally a felicitous synthesis of the two. Hardly anybody believes that this is the way that history has been or will turn out, but it is worth broaching a few of the reasons why it sounds so implausible. For one thing, we know that there never was a golden age. But it is true, even so, that 'traditional' or pre-modern societies have a great many merits which our own set-ups lack, and in some cases have these merits just because they don't have what we have. On the whole they have a richer sense of place, community and tradition, less social anomie, less cut-throat competition and tormented ambition, less subjection to a ruthlessly instrumental rationality and so on. On the other hand, and for much the same reasons, they are often desperately impoverished, culturally claustrophobic, socially hidebound and patriarchal, and without much sense of the autonomous individual. Modernity has precisely such a sense of free individual development, with all the spiritual wealth that this brings with it; it also begins to hatch notions of human equality and universal rights largely unknown to its forebears. But we also know that this is the more civilized face of a barbarously uncaring order, one which sunders all significant relations between its members, deprives them of precious symbolic resources and persuades them to mistake the means of life for the ends of it. We also know that the two forms of social life share a depressing amount in common: hard labour, oppression and exploitation, ferocious power-struggles, lethal mythologies, military violence and the rest. To this extent, neither romantic nostalgia nor modernist triumphalism are in the least appealing. But neither are romantic anti-capitalism or a modernist contempt for tradition.

It is this, surely, which the utopian narrative of a condition which combined the best of both worlds is groping for. It may not be a feasible future, but at least it issues a salutary warning against both despair and presumption, blinkered reaction and callow progressivism. To dream of blending the best of both worlds is also to refuse the worst of both. This is not a vision especially dear to the hearts of postmodernists, but one needs to ask why not. Are they saying that they are not really captivated by the thought of a society which managed somehow to reinvent a degree of human reciprocity at the level of developed individual powers, or just that they think the idea is ludicrously abstract, historically impossible and so really not worth bothering about? They might well have a point here; but if they are saying the former, then one feels stirred to ask why they find this prospect so oddly uninspiring. For it is hard in my view to imagine a more desirable human condition, quite regardless of whether it could ever come about. It is, more or less, what Marx had in mind by communism, in which the individual would finally come into her own. There is no teleology in the sense that this state of affairs is even now shadowily present at the end of history, waiting patiently for us to catch up with it. But it would not, after all, be a bad sort of teleology to keep it in mind, as a heuristic fiction or Kantian 'idea', in the midst of our political action, provided we avoided the *hubris* and false utopia of trying to beam our actions directly at it.

Teleology usually involves the assumption that there is some potential in the present which could result in a particular sort of future. But this need not mean that this potential lurks within the present like petals within a bud. It is present rather in the sense that I have a potential to travel up to Glasgow right now, which is hardly some kind of secret structure of my being. Teleology here is just a way of describing where I am in the light of where I could feasibly get to. It shows how a future which transcends the present is also a function of it, though not in some fatalistic sense. I have a train ticket to Glasgow, something produced in this country which could in principle get me out of it, but there is no assurance that I shall use it. This brings us, finally, to a different sense of teleology, which we can touch on only briefly. This is a meaning which concerns the individual rather than the historical, and is to be found in Aristotle's discussion of the good life. Aristotle's ethics are not of the modern kind, centred in Kantian style on concepts of duty, the solitary moral subject and the rightness or wrongness of its isolable actions. They focus rather upon the idea of virtue, which is to say upon the shape, texture and quality of a whole life in its practical social context. Virtue is a matter of the proper, pleasurable fulfilment of one's human powers, both a practice and a matter of practise. Being human is a set of techniques, something you have to get good at like tolerating bores or playing the harmonica, and you cannot do it on your own any more than you could carry out major surgery simply by instinct. These are teleological ideas in so far as they involve the trajectory of a whole life in its appropriate unfolding; whereas postmodernism, like David Hume, doubts that there is that much continuity in human selves. Whatever one thinks of that, these are richly suggestive notions which the anaemic morality of modernity disastrously left behind with its fetishes of duty, imperatives, prohibitions, the suppression of pleasure and the like. Which is not to suggest that such ideas have no place in moral discourse (many prohibitions are progressive), just that the few forays which postmodernism has so far made into the field of ethics have been depressingly reliant on this Kantian terminology. Just as some mechanistic Marxists of the Second International turned incongruously to Kant for their moral values because it was proving impossible to generate those values out of their positivist views of history, so postmodernism, which has its own brand of positivism, not least in its wariness of metaphysical depth, seems to have taken to repeating the gesture. And in this sense too it is a child of the modernity it claims to have superseded.

The rejection of so-called metanarratives is definitive of postmodern philosophy, but the options it poses here are sometimes rather narrow. Either you are enthused by a particular metanarrative, such as the story of technological progress or the march of Mind, or you find these fables oppressive and turn instead to a plurality of tales. But we have seen already that these are not the only choices available, as indeed the more intelligent postmodernist recognizes. Socialism holds to a sort of metanarrative, but it is by no means the kind of bed-time story one would recount to a child given to nightmares. It has its more upbeat aspects, but in other ways it is a horror story. The sooner it is over the better; it is just that proclaiming it over already, as postmodernists tend to do, is likely to help perpetuate it.

The other misleading choice offered by some (though not all) postmodernism is to imagine that there is either a single metanarrative or a multiplicity of micronarratives. The same goes for the postmodern concept of foundations: either there is one of them, or none at all.[6] This all-or-nothingism ill befits a supposedly non-binary theory. What if there were a plurality of metanarratives? There are basically two kinds of activity which keep the human species going, one of them to do with material reproduction and the other with sexual reproduction. Without these two stories, human history would have ground to a halt and postmodernism would have nothing to be posterior to. And both of these stories have been chronicles of ceaseless warfare. To call them 'metanarratives' is not to suggest that they each encompass everything that ever happened (how could either, since we already have two of them?), or that some unruptured thread of continuity runs through them both, or that they are in every respect the most valuable or interesting tales one can tell. Interesting in what sense? They may be what keep the species going, but they are both fairly sordid anecdotes, and for value one would be well advised to turn to culture, which in its narrower sense is not central to the survival of the species at all. There would, to be sure, be no culture at all without these grander chronicles, but that makes them more fundamental than culture only in the sense that Dickens's having a pen was fundamental to *Little Dorrit*. These particular *grands récits* are significant for two reasons:

first, because they are the cause today as in the past of a good deal of misery which needs to be put to rights, and secondly because if we do not do so they shall go on demanding enormous investments of energy and hence distract us from the pleasures of talking about something more interesting for a change. These stories bulk so large in our lives, precisely because they have proved so problematic, that they weigh burdensomely upon many of our micronarratives too, skewing them from the inside and leaving their bleak inscription upon them. If one wanted a fresh understanding of the Marxist model of base and superstructure, one could perhaps find it here.

These are not metanarratives in the sense of being stories of which all other stories are a mere function. Marxism has very little of interest to say about the virtues of Icelandic cuisine in contrast to Bulgarian. Why should it? It is not some sort of cosmic philosophy along the lines of Rosicrucianism. It has had fairly little of interest to say about feminism either, partly because much of it has been conventionally patriarchal, but also because it is a restricted narrative which was never intended to be a Theory of Everything. It is not a fault of feminist theory that it has made few major contributions to Marxist thought; why should it have done? There is a difference between a theory from which everything else can be supposedly deduced, as in the more megalomaniac forms of high rationalism, and a narrative which is 'grand' in the sense of providing the matrix within which many, but not all, of our other practices take shape. And there are, arguably, other grand narratives besides the ones I have mentioned, such as the global story of imperialism and colonialism. In denying that this constitutes a metanarrative, one should be careful as a Westerner that one is not subtly defusing it. It is curious that so much postcolonial theory should want to deny the systematic, world-historical nature of the imperial history it examines, its repetitions as well as its differences, thus in some sense letting it off the hook. But none of these fables is 'grand' because it operates by a single logic, any more than *Middlemarch* does.

Postmodernism, wedded as it is to the particular, would be reluctant to accept that there are propositions which are true of all times and places, yet which are not simply vacuous or trivial. The statement 'In all times and places, most men and women have led lives of fairly futile labour, usually for the profit of a few' seems one such utterance. 'Women have always suffered oppression' is another. To narrativize these propositions is to help defamiliarize them – to recover something of our naive astonishment at what we had taken for granted. There is a sense in which we can forget or deny what is most common exactly because it *is* so common, as in Roland Barthes's celebrated example of those names of countries which march across the map in such huge capitals that they are effectively invisible. Grand narratives are in this sense a bit like transcendental conditions, so much the very framework of our perception that it is hard to stare at them straight.

Similarly, it is difficult for us to recapture the imaginative excitement which must have burst upon the world with the concept of universality. What could have sounded more scandalous to a profoundly particularist culture, one in which what you were was bound up with your region, function, social rank, than the extraordinary notion that everyone was entitled to individual respect quite independently of these things? This outlandish new doctrine was of course launched into philosophical orbit from a highly specific position, that of a wing of the European bourgeoisie, but so is every doctrine, universal or otherwise. Whether Jean Baudrillard's ideas are true or false is not to be determined by the fact that he is a Frenchman working in California, even if these facts may have some relevance to their formation. The exotic new thesis was abroad that you were entitled to freedom, autonomy, justice, happiness, political equality and the rest not because you were the son of a minor Prussian count but simply on account of your humanity. We now had rights, obligations and responsibilities which put in brackets all of our most intimately individuating features. Postmodernism is in general allergic to any such trampling on the particular, and this ferocious abstraction trampled on it with a vengeance. It was also one of the greatest emancipatory ideas of world history, one which postmodernism has come so much to take for granted that it can apparently only identify it by its blindspots. It was not at all true in practice that everyone – women, for example, or non-Europeans or the lower peasantry – was accorded equal respect. But everyone's freedom mattered in theory, and 'in theory' is a sizeable improvement on its not mattering even as that. It is an improvement not least because middle-class society could now be challenged by those it suppressed *according to its own logic*, caught out in a performative contradiction between what it said and what it did. And this is always a far sharper form of critique than measuring a social order against values whose validity it would not even acknowledge.

This great revolutionary concept was of course thoroughly essentialist. It was by virtue of our shared human nature that we had ethical and political claims upon one another, not for any more parochial, paternalist or sheerly cultural reason. These matters were too important to be left to the tender mercies of custom or tradition, to the whim of your masters or the tacit codes of your community. The respect you had been contingently granted could be just as contingently withdrawn, and this was too feeble a basis for an ethics. Justice had to be indifferent; it was the *anciens régimes* which were the great apologists for difference, in the sense that how you were treated depended on how you were ranked. Difference was now a reactionary idea, and sameness or identity a revolutionary one. If you wanted to reject elitism or autocracy on anything stronger than pragmatic grounds, you had to go universalist. Postmodernism, which tends to both anti-elitism and anti-universalism,[7] thus lives a certain tension between its political and philosophical values. It seeks to resolve this by short-circuiting universality and returning in a sense of premodern particularism, but now to a particularism without privilege, which is to say to a difference without hierarchy. Its problem is how a difference without hierarchy is not to collapse into pure *in*difference, so becoming a kind of inverted mirror-image of the universalism it repudiates.

This universality must apply to ethics too. One kind of postmodern sceptic of universality believes in culturalist style that moral values are just embedded in contingent local traditions, and have no more force than that. An egregious example of this case is the American philosopher Richard Rorty, who in an essay entitled 'Solidarity' argues that those who helped Jews in the last world war probably did so less because they saw them as fellow human beings but because they belonged to the same city, profession or other social grouping as themselves. He then goes on to ask himself why modern American liberals should help oppressed American blacks. 'Do we say that these people must be helped because they are our fellow human beings? We may, but it is much more persuasive, morally as well as politically, to describe them as our fellow *Americans* – to insist that it is outrageous that an *American* should live without hope.'[8] Morality, in short, is really just a species of patriotism.

Rorty's case, however, strikes me as still too universalist. There are, after all, rather a lot of Americans, of various shapes and sizes, and there is surely something a little abstract in basing one's compassion on such grandiosely general grounds. It is almost as though 'America' operates here as some sort of metalanguage or metaphysical essence, collapsing into unity a vast variety of creeds, lifestyles, ethnic groupings and so on. Would it not be preferable for an authentic critic of universality to base his fellow-feeling on some genuine localism, say the city block? On second thoughts, however, this is still a little on the homogenizing side, since your average city block does of course contain a fair sprinkling of different sorts of people; but it would surely be a more manageable basis for social justice than some universal abstraction like America. One might demonstrate compassion to those in the next apartment, for example, while withholding it from those down the street. Personally, I only ever display sympathy to fellow graduates of the University of Cambridge. It is true that such credentials aren't always easy to establish: I have occasionally tossed a coin towards some tramp whom I thought I recognized as a member of the class of 1964, only to retrieve it furtively again when I realized my mistake. But the alternatives to such a strategy are fairly dire. Once one begins extending compassion to graduates of Oxford too, there seems no reason not to go on to Sheffield, Warwick and the Lower Bumpstead College of Agricultural Science, and before one knows where one is one is on the slippery slope to universalism, foundationalism, Jürgen Habermas and the rest.

I have not, incidentally, yet resigned from the Campaign for Nuclear Disarmament, merely adjusted my reasons for belonging. I now object to nuclear warfare not because it would blow up some metaphysical abstraction known as the human race, but because it would introduce a degree of unpleasantness into the lives of my Oxford neighbours. The benefit of this adjustment is that my membership of the campaign is no longer the bloodless, cerebral affair it once was, but pragmatic, experiential, lived sensuously on the pulses. If my bit of Oxford survives a nuclear catastrophe, I really couldn't care less about the University of Virginia.

Rorty, commendably enough, really does seem to believe that getting rid of pointless abstractions like 'universal humanity' would actually allow us to be more morally and politically effective. He is not so much opposed to them because they are false, a kind of judgement he does not much relish making in the first place, as because they are distractions from the true tasks in hand. He would need, however, to find grounds for distancing himself from the kind of anti-universalist who believed that murder was wrong for everyone except for aristocrats who were above the law, benighted heathens who knew no better, and those whose time-hallowed traditions happened to sanction it. It is this kind of privilege which the Enlightenment was trying to counter, and it is surely a case with strong intuitive force. In theory if not always in practice, it provided you with a powerful counterblast to those paternally minded colonialists who thought that the natives weren't up to moral virtue or simply had ideas of it which failed to mesh with their own. The idea of human emancipation is part of the progeny of Enlightenment, and those radical postmodernists who mobilize it are inevitably in debt to their antagonists. In a similar way, the Enlightenment itself inherited concepts of universal justice and equality from a Judaeo-Christian tradition which it frequently derided. Universality just means that, when it comes to freedom, justice and happiness, everyone has to be in on the act.

In on whose act, however? That of white Western males who assume that their own idiosyncratic version of humanity should apply to everyone else? This is certainly one of the primary ways in which the idea of universality has been touted, and the postmodern objection to it is to that extent perfectly just. It is just typically unpluralistic of postmodernists to imagine that this is *all* that universality can mean. Postmodernists fear that such universalism will simply ride roughshod over cultural difference, and there is plenty of evidence that they are right. But universality and difference are not necessarily at odds. Take, for example, the concept of human equality. You can understand this as meaning that all people are equal in their concrete attributes, which is clearly fatuous: some people are a lot finer or shabbier than others, in particular respects. Or you can see it, along with the liberals, as meaning that everyone must have an equal opportunity of becoming unequal. This fails to capture our strong intuition that human equality goes deeper down than this, to do in some obscure way with what some socialists have called 'equality of being'. A character in D. H. Lawrence's novel *Aaron's Rod* plaintively suggests that all human beings are equal in their souls, only to be brusquely informed that this is where they are least equal. What, then, does it mean to treat two individuals equally? It cannot surely mean treating them the same, since if these individuals have different needs and capacities this is bound to issue in injustice. It was for this reason that Marx, in *The Critique of the Gotha Programme* and elsewhere, regarded the notion of equality as a typical bourgeois abstraction, one which was secretly modelled on the exchanges of the commodity form. Socialism is not in the end much interested in equality. To treat two people equally must surely mean not giving them exactly the same treatment but attending equally to their different needs. It is not that they are equal individuals, but that they are equally individuals. And to this extent a reasonable concept of equality already implicates the notion of difference.

This mutual implication is apparent in other ways too. Marx strongly believed in a common or universal human nature, but he considered individuation to be an integral part of it. It is a peculiarity of our species that we are so constituted as to live our natures differentially – not just in the sense that there are no two exactly identical tomatoes, but in the sense that this individuation is an *activity* of our 'species being'. It belongs to our species life to bring ourselves into being, through others, as unique individuals. Difference is natural to us; and if we wanted an example of this constant interplay of individuality and universality, we need only turn to the phenomenon of language.[9] But difference and universality are also mutually implicated in the sense that, for classical liberalism, universality exists finally for the *sake* of difference. Confronted with the 'given' differences of human beings, we must first abstract from these specificities so that all of them end up with equal political rights. But the point of that abstraction is to move us to a 'higher' stage of difference, in which all individuals will now have the freedom, protection and resources they need to develop in their own different ways.

This is an admirable ideal, even though, as socialists point out, the ironic upshot of these actual differences, in class society, is continually to break down the very basis of equality from which they evolved. People will be abstractly levelled at the legal and political levels only to be vastly unequal at the social and economic ones. Because individual development in this sort of set-up is inseparable from the exploitation of others, a point the liberal refuses to recognize, it will prove a curiously self-scuppering kind of social order. As the immanent critique of this culture, Marxism applauds its great universalist ideals, to which it knows itself to be enduringly indebted. Unlike some modern-day radicals, 'bourgeois' for Marx does not automatically mean 'bad', which would be just the sort of abstract, unhistorical bit of moralism that modern-day radicals are supposed to disapprove of. At the same time, though, Marxism is out to show how in practice these fine ideals tend to crush all sensuous specificity beneath their heel. There is no final quarrel between Marxism and postmodernism on the question of difference: Marx's whole political ethic is devoted to releasing sensuous particularity, or the full richness of individual powers, from the metaphysical prison-houses of abstraction. It is just that he recognizes that if *everyone's* unique difference is to be respected, this ethic must be universally extended, a process which then necessarily involves abstraction.

Socialists, or at least Marxists, are often hotly upbraided with being universalists. But while this is true in one sense, it is false in another. One is a socialist, among other reasons, precisely because universality *doesn't* exist at present in any positive, as opposed to merely descriptive or ideological, sense. Not everyone, as yet, enjoys freedom, happiness and justice. Part of what prevents this from coming about is precisely the false universalism which holds that it can be achieved by extending the values and liberties of a particular sector of humankind, roughly speaking Western Man, to the entire globe. The myth of the 'end of history' is the complacent belief that this has either now happened or is well on the way to happening. Socialism is a critique of this false universalism, not in the name of a cultural particularism which is often enough simply its other face, but in the name of the right of everyone to negotiate their own difference in terms of everyone else's. And in this ceaseless transaction, nobody's *present* differences can be guaranteed to survive, which is hardly music to the ears of certain militant particularisms of our day. In this sense, socialism deconstructs the current oppositions between universal reason and culture-bound practices, abstract rights and concrete affiliations, liberalism and communitarianism, Enlightenment nature and postmodern culture. The answer to whether the world is growing more global or more local is surely a resounding yes; but these two dimensions are currently deadlocked, each pushing the other into a monstrous parody of itself, as transnational corporations which know no homeland confront ethnic nationalisms which know nothing else. To redefine the relations between difference and universality is thus more than a theoretical exercise; it may well be the index of any worthwhile political future.

A certain kind of old-style hierarchical conservative, not much in evidence these days, believes that 'given' differences between human beings should be directly translated into political terms: those who have the finest qualities of leadership should rule. Almost everyone now appreciates that this view simply skates over how little 'given' such qualities actually are. The liberal's case is rather more complex: 'given' inequalities must first be artificially evened up by the apparatus of the state, so that everyone has more or less the same chance as everyone else; but this will then result, in a third stage, in the flowering of a wealth of difference and individuality. Liberalism thus presses a stage further than old-style conservatism; but it also goes a stage further than much postmodernism. As far as these issues go, postmodernism is neither liberal nor conservative but *libertarian*, though strangely, as we have seen, a libertarianism without much of a subject to be liberated. Unlike liberalism, it wants a difference which is not filtered through universality to emerge somewhere on the other side of it, since it fears that such differences will simply be eradicated *en route*. But since it wants to multiply difference all over the place, it is hard to see how this is not just a kind of shamefaced universalism. To argue that you want to fashion a society in which everybody is incommensurate with everyone else is inevitably to make a totalizing, universalist claim. It is, incidentally, a claim which is the merest commonplace of Romanticism, and thus not so much postmodernist as pre-modernist. Such libertarians are simply unable to say how the proliferating of differences would apply all round without involving themselves in the very discourses which they regard as inimical to this goal. It is for this reason that the more sophisticated sort of postmodern theorist will not, indeed cannot reject universalism outright; Jacques Derrida is by no means simply opposed to Enlightenment, and neither was the later Michel Foucault.

Socialists and postmodernists are agreed that the concept of difference finally travels beyond ideas of both equality and inequality. It was D. H. Lawrence, of all people, who remarked that when he was in the presence of another human being he experienced neither equality nor inequality, but simply otherness. But that, as it stands, could be true of one's response to the presence of a slave, who is unlikely to feel *your* presence simply as 'other'. The libertarian can't get as far as bourgeois democracy, whereas the liberal can't get beyond it. What both creeds have in common, however, is that they each value difference as their final ideal, different though those differences may be. And this is where both of them differ from socialism. For socialism, difference is not the final political goal, even if it is part of that goal, and inseparable from its attainment. A politics based upon difference alone will be unable to advance very far beyond traditional liberalism – and indeed quite a bit of postmodernism, with its zest for plurality, multiplicity, provisionality, anti-totality, open-endedness and the rest, has the look of a sheepish liberalism in wolf's clothing. The political goal of socialism is not a resting in difference, which is then just the flipside of a spurious universalism, but the emancipation of difference at the level of human mutuality or reciprocity. And this would be indispensable for the discovery or creation of our real differences, which can only in the end be explored in reciprocal ways, and which may then well turn out to be different from what we currently consider them to be. It seems to me that we cannot now describe exactly what political forms will enable this process, trapped as we are between a vacuous universalism and a myopic particularism. Indeed it is a sign of that dilemma that when theorists like Adorno come to imagine a new form of totality, which would enhance rather than violate the sensuously specific, they have

and being gloomily fatalistic. Much postmodernism has sprung from the United States, or at least has taken rapid root there, and reflects some of that country's most intractable political problems. It is then perhaps a little ethnocentric of this anti-ethnocentrism, though hardly a gesture unknown to that nation, to project its own political backyard onto the world at large. There is now an institute for postmodern studies at the University of Beijing, as China imports Derrida along with Diet Coke.[10] If postmodernism is a form of culturalism, it is because among other reasons it refuses to recognize that what different ethnic groups have in common socially and economically is finally more important than their cultural differences. More important for what? For the purposes of their political emancipation. There is no question that these groups are the victims of racism as well as capitalism, and no question either of anti-racists and anti-capitalists vying with each other over which of these is the more fundamental. This would be just another depressing instance of the way that much radical academia in the United States has managed to translate urgent political issues into its own blandly professional terms, so that conflicts beyond the campuses become transposed in unseemly fashion into tussles over defending or promoting academic patches, fighting off radical competitors in the intellectual marketplace, securing funds for this rather than that avant-garde enterprise. The left has always had an infallible knack of tearing itself apart before the political enemy could lay a glove on it. It is rather a question of claiming that ethnic groups which were able to unite with each other over their common material exploitation, without thereby sinking their cultural differences, would stand a far better chance of dismantling the system which holds them all down than any set of discrete 'community' demands. Such community demands are of course crucial; but you cannot, for example, raise the issues of property ownership and control in a purely local idiom. The fact that such a project is for the moment simply not on in the United States, or for that matter anywhere else, is no reason to stymie it even further by denying its importance. Culturalism is an occupational hazard of literary intellectuals, and has slotted marvellously well into a certain reading of the current political situation of the West. But those political conflicts are not in the end about culture, however vital culture undoubtedly is to those seeking to reclaim their identities and inheritances. It is because of its commitment to minorities that postmodernism questions the notion of a general humanity; but it is difficult to see how some such appeal would not be necessary for defending minorities against racist assault.

Culturalism in our time has also taken the form of cultural relativism, as an understandable overreaction to a dubious-looking universal rationality. (When one emphasizes, as Jacques Derrida once remarked, one always overemphasizes.) One might begin by putting in a word or two for rationality itself, since whereas some postmodernists are chary of a universal rationality, some of them are just chary of rationality. It is little wonder that they are, in an era when its instrumental variety has inflated out of all proportion. One might expect in such a period that some would begin to confuse objectivity with objectivism, or scientific enquiry with scientism. (Though postmodern culture has its own aesthetic equivalent of scientism, in the work of art's notorious 'absence of affect'.) Objectivity means among other things a decentred openness to the reality of others, and as Platonists see is in its more affective reaches closely linked with love. The fact that this is probably in any full sense impossible should not deter us from trying it on. Reason at its best is related to generosity, to being able to acknowledge the truth or justice of another's claim even when it cuts against the grain of one's own interests and desires. To be reasonable in this sense involves not some desiccated calculation but courage, realism, justice, humility and largesse of spirit; there is certainly nothing clinically disinterested about it. Objectivity in its more useful senses refers to the status of certain kinds of truth-claim or the nature of certain sorts of speech act. I tell you that it has been a terrible day and you take this as some sort of subjective utterance, meaning that I just happen to feel vaguely out of sorts. You take what I say as you might take: 'Whenever I hear that Mozart concerto, I always think of boot polish.' But registering your category mistake, I point out that my statement was intended to have objective force. It has been a bad day because my daughter has just scampered off with all my savings to open a night-club in Amsterdam. I may actually turn out to be wrong; she was just down at the corner shop after all. But my statement was intended objectively in any case.

Cultural relativism at its most embattled imagines that different cultures are wholly self-validating and mutually incommensurable. Even if there were some sort of rationality in common between them, it would first have to be translated into both cultures' entirely different terms and so, presuming that they could identify it at all, would instantly cease to offer common ground. Hardly anyone actually responds like this when they run into someone from another culture; nobody actually behaves as though there was *nothing* in common between them, whatever the daunting difficulties of mutual dialogue. But the case has stubbornly survived its empirical implausibility. If cultures are internally self-validating, then it would be sheer imperial arrogance for our own culture to seek to pass judgement on any other. But by the same token these other cultures could not pass judgement on ours. The corollary of not being able to tell someone anything is that they can tell you nothing either. Postmodern 'anti-ethnocentrism' thus leaves our own culture conveniently insulated from anyone else's critique. All those anti-Western bleatings from the so-called third world may safely be ignored, since they are interpreting our conduct in terms quite irrelevant to us.

There is yet another sense, relevant to culturalism, in which the particular and the universal are not necessarily at odds. Cultures can be criticized by universalist criteria not only from the standpoint of some other culture, but from within themselves. As Charles Taylor puts it, this 'moral outlook . . . engenders a pitiless criticism of all those beliefs and practices within our society which fail to meet the standard of universal respect'.[11] It is not just a question of intervening into other people's cultures, but of intervening into our own. Feminists in Belgium or Borneo who protest that women there are excluded from full humanity are making precisely such an appeal. As for 'ethnocentrism', we now find ourselves plunged into the faintly farcical situation of guiltily disowning Western ideas at the very moment when one or two of them might prove of some use to political critics in the neo-colonial world. The legacy of colonialism has so understandably sickened all good Western liberals or postmodernists that in an access of cultural self-loathing they are rushing to deconstruct some of the very notions which might come in useful for those their own histories have for so long held down. This is not of course to suggest that neo-colonial political opposition should obediently conform to Western Enlightenment, which has been at least as much part of the problem as of the solution. But Western radicals who find their own culture of little or no value, and who consequently look askance on the possibility of pieces of it being found valuable by others, take a curiously reverential attitude towards Western ideas. It is as though they could not imagine these ideas being transformed, reworked, radically refunctioned, just as some of their conservative antagonists cannot. They miss the force of Bertolt Brecht's implicit slogan: 'Use what you can, and if you can't, don't', or of Walter Benjamin's tactic recommendation: 'Collect all you can because you never know when it might come in handy.' Who is cocksure enough to predict that medieval love poetry might not prove a more precious resource in some political struggle than the writings of Surrealist Trotskyists? Are radicals really so wedded to the idea of the fixed meaning of the text? What an insult to the working people of the West, whose labour lay at the source of those cultures, to inform them airily that they are nothing but oppressive! And how conveniently such histrionic gestures serve to reinforce forms of ethnocentrism in the so-called third world itself, thus merely exporting the beast from one sphere to another.

The idea of universality involves the concept of identity: for certain political purposes, but by no means for all purposes, individuals must be treated alike. 'Identity' here means, for example, that you have no right to greater political authority than I have just because your father happens to be Lord Lieutenant of Shropshire. Yet identity is one of the great bugbears of postmodern thought, in an age when too many people languish for the lack of it. Low self-esteem is as widespread as poor eyesight, and a lot more disabling. It is our rulers who do not need to identify themselves with any certainty because they falsely assume that they know precisely who they are. A reasonably secure identity, as against a paranoically cohesive one, is a necessary condition of human well-being, and those postmodernists who fail to mention this fact are being morally irresponsible. Neither a subject which cannot name itself at all, nor one which can name itself only too well, is likely to be an effective agent of social transformation.

What postmodernism pits against identity, in the sense of sameness, is plurality, which it oddly assumes to be an unequivocally positive good. In her study *Contingencies of Value*, Barbara Hernstein Smith argues that 'it is perhaps just as well for "our society" that its norms are a "melange", that they constantly multiply, collide, and transform each other, that conflicts of judgement are negotiated *ad hoc*, and that normative authority is itself multiple and recurrently changes hands, variously strengthening and becoming diffuse.'[12] It is interesting to observe those scare-quotes nervously shielding the phrase 'our society', as the author finds herself forced into a totalization she might otherwise disown. One had not previously been aware that the United States was some sort of carnivalesque utopia, but it is gratifying to learn that all one had heard about racial conflict, religious fundamentalism, corporate power and patriarchal reaction was simply red propaganda.[13] One wonders if Latin American political activists have yet got round to appreciating the humble, *ad hoc* way in which the USA resolves conflicts of political judgement, or whether the gun lobby reveals a postmodern *mélange* of ceaselessly variable norms. Hernstein Smith, along with almost all postmodern theorists, would seem to imagine that difference, variability and heterogeneity are 'absolute' goods, and it is a position I have long held myself. It has always struck me as unduly impoverishing of British social life that we can muster a mere two or three fascist parties. We also seem stuck with far too few social classes, whereas if the postmodern imperative to multiply differences were to be taken literally we should strive to breed as many more of them as we could, say two or three new bourgeoisies and a fresh clutch of landowning aristocracies.

The opinion that plurality[14] is a good in itself is emptily formalistic and alarmingly unhistorical. So is the view that identity is negative in itself. Postmodernism tends to be dogmatically monistic about pluralism, which is of course *very often* a good, but by no means always. One would have expected that the pragmatically-minded might have been a touch more contextual about their claims. A great deal of postmodern politics is based on an opposition between identity and otherness: what is to be fundamentally rejected, 'absolutely' one might be tempted to say, is the dominion of self-identity over otherness and difference. This political ethic has spoken with impressive eloquence to certain kinds of contemporary political conflict; but taken overall it is drastically partial and simplistic. Is *all* violent exclusion of the other to be upbraided? Kicking the British out of India, or the Portuguese out of Angola? How does it address itself to exploitative situations – the office labour of Birmingham, for example, or the sweatshops of South East Asia – where there is no particularly dramatic confrontation between identity and otherness? Or is postmodernism once more modelling all political situations on its own most privileged ones, in violation of its own pluralist tenets? Catholics and Protestants in Northern Ireland in some ways confront each other as alien and fear the dissolution of their own cultural identities by the contamination of the other. This is the aspect of the situation which postmodernism is good at grasping, but usually the only aspect. In other ways, however, Northern Irish Catholics and Protestants are not culturally alien to each other at all: they share pretty much the same kind of working-class culture, with certain important religious variants, and in general understand each other only too well. The Northern Irish conflict has something to do with cultural identity, but a great deal more to do with a contention between two groups who owe allegiance to different political states. There is of course an ethnic and cultural context to those clashing political affinities, but it is by no means decisive. Ulster Protestants do not on the whole wish to remain British because they dread as cultural interlopers people who speak Irish or say the rosary, but because by doing so they can maintain their political hegemony, along with a higher standard of living. The latter point is the kind of argument that some postmodernists would label 'economistic', despite a claim to be 'materialist'.

Universality is not just an ideological illusion. On the contrary, it is the single most palpable feature of our political world. It is not just an idea one can choose or oppose as the theoretical fancy takes you, but the structure of global reality itself. As Justin Rosenberg writes: 'By the end of the twentieth century . . . the wilfulness lies patently with anyone who seeks to deny the need for large-scale, systematic, historical explanation. For this has been an age of global wars, of ideological conflicts superimposed on a global state system, of booms and slumps that were worldwide in their impact, and of (ecological and political) challenges which now confront the whole of humanity.'[15] We must ask ourselves why it is, then, that just at the historical moment when this system was becoming more 'total' than ever, some radical intellectuals began to denounce the whole notion of totality as a bad dream. Was it among other things because, fixated on fascism or Stalinism, the only kind of totality they could imagine was the crudely obvious one of 'totalitarianism'? As the environmentalists are only too aware, universality in the end means that we inhabit the same small planet; and though we may forget about totality, we may be sure that it will not forget about us.

We come finally to 'humanist', a term bedevilled by its several clashing meanings. There is an ethical sense of the word, meaning the belief that human beings should be accorded compassion and respect; a sociological sense, meaning that social structures are best viewed as the products of human agents; and an historical sense, denoting periods such as the Renaissance in which 'man' becomes the centre of scholarly attention. This latter meaning may or may not involve yet another sense of the term: the belief that there is an important distinction between humans and other animals, perhaps, though not necessarily, with the corollary that the former should rule sovereign over the latter. But the word can also suggest the sovereignty of the human as opposed to the divine or supernatural, in which case it becomes a rather more positive synonym for atheism or agnosticism, and merges into the idea of a 'naturalistic' world view. For this Enlightenment doctrine, it belongs to the dignity of human beings that they should rely upon their own capacities, rather than on some transcendent power. This in turn may be coupled with a further meaning of 'humanist' – an affirmation of human self-development or self-perfection, usually with progressivist or even utopian implications. Such a belief, however, need not be anti-supernaturalist, as in the case of the various Christian humanisms of the West.

It is clear that one can be a humanist in some of these senses but not in others. Almost nobody is anti-humanist in the sense of urging that other people should be boiled alive, though quite a lot of people are anti-humanist in the sense of considering that human agents are best seen as the products of social systems rather than as the producers of them. You can be a humanist in the sense of finding no value in God, but anti-humanist in finding no value in human beings either. Indeed this is a typically conservative estimate of humanity, one shared by the more apocalyptic brands of ecology. You can, like Spinoza, be a philosophical anti-humanist in the sense of denying freedom of will and regarding human beings as the effects of some inexorable determinism, while remaining, again like Spinoza, a devout humanist as far as the ethical life goes. Or you may place particular value on humanity without

6

Contradictions

The chief contradiction of postmodernism is a little like that of old-fashioned structuralism. Was structuralism radical or conservative? It is easy enough to see the ways in which it behaved as a kind of technocracy of the spirit, the final penetration of the rationalizing impulse of modernity into the inner sanctum of the subject. With its rigorous codings, universal schemas and hard-nosed reductionism, it reflected in the sphere of *Geist* a reification already apparent in reality. But this is only one side of the story. For in extending the logic of technocracy into the mind, structuralism scandalized the liberal humanism whose task was to preserve the life of the mind from any such vulgar reduction. And this liberal humanism was one of the dominant ideologies of technocratic society itself. In this sense, structuralism was radical and conservative at the same time, colluding with the strategies of modern capitalism in a way deeply at odds with its own sovereign values. It is as though by pressing a sort of technological determinism all the way through to the mind itself, treating individuals as the mere empty locus of impersonal codes, it imitated the way modern society actually treats them but pretends it does not, thus endorsing its logic while unmasking its ideals. 'System', writes Roland Barthes, 'is the enemy of Man' – meaning, no doubt, that for humanism the subject is always that which is radically irreducible, that which will seep through the cracks of your categories and play havoc with your structures.

There is a similar sort of contradiction built into postmodernism, which is also both radical and conservative together. It is a striking feature of advanced capitalist societies that they are both libertarian and authoritarian, hedonistic and repressive, multiple and monolithic. And the reason for this is not hard to find. The logic of the marketplace is one of pleasure and plurality, of the ephemeral and discontinuous, of some great decentred network of desire of which individuals seem the mere fleeting effects. Yet to hold all this potential anarchy in place requires strong foundations and a firm political framework. The more market forces threaten to subvert all stability, the more stridently one will need to insist upon traditional values. It is not unusual to find British politicians who support the commercialization of radio but are horrified by poems which don't rhyme. But the more this system appeals to metaphysical values to legitimate itself, the more its own rationalizing, secularizing activities threaten to strike them hollow. These regimes can neither abandon the metaphysical nor properly accommodate it, and they are thus always potentially self-deconstructing.

The political ambivalences of postmodernism match this contradiction exactly. One might venture, in a first crude approximation, that a lot of postmodernism is politically oppositional but economically complicit. This, however, requires some fine tuning. Postmodernism is radical in so far as it challenges a system which still needs absolute values, metaphysical foundations and self-identical subjects; against these it mobilizes multiplicity, non-identity, transgression, anti-foundationalism, cultural relativism. The result, at its best, is a resourceful subversion of the dominant value-system, at least at the level of theory. There are business executives who have heard all about deconstruction and react to it much as religious fundamentalists do to atheism. In fact they are quite right to do so, since in its more politicized forms deconstruction is indeed an assault on much of what most businessmen hold dear. But postmodernism usually fails to recognize that what goes at the level of ideology does not always go at the level of the market.

If the system has need of the autonomous subject in the law court or polling booth, it has little enough use for it in the media or shopping mall. In these sectors, plurality, desire, fragmentation and the rest are as native to the way we live as coal was to Newcastle before Margaret Thatcher got her hands on it. Many a business executive is in this sense a spontaneous postmodernist. Capitalism is the most pluralistic order history has ever known, restlessly transgressing boundaries and dismantling oppositions, pitching together diverse life-forms and continually overflowing the measure. The whole of this plurality, need one say, operates within quite stringent limits; but it helps to explain why some postmodernists look eagerly to a hybridized future while others are persuaded that it has already arrived.

Postmodernism, in short, scoops up something of the material logic of advanced capitalism and turns this aggressively against its spiritual foundations. And in this it bears more than a passing resemblance to the structuralism which was one of its remote sources. It is as though it is urging the system, like its great mentor Friedrich Nietzsche, to forget about its metaphysical foundations, acknowledge that God is dead and simply go relativist. Then, at least, it might trade a modicum of security for a degree of actuality. Why not just confess that your values are as precariously ungrounded as anybody else's? It would hardly leave you vulnerable to attack, since you have just craftily demolished any vantage-point from which any offensive might be launched. In any case, the kind of values which are rooted in what you do, which reflect the unvarnished social reality rather than the high-falutin moral ideal, are likely to be a good deal more cogent than a lot of nebulous talk about progress, reason or God's special affection for the nation.

But it is all very well for pragmatist philosophers to argue in this way. Those who bear the burden of running the system are aware that ideologies are in business to *legitimate* what you do, not just to reflect it. They cannot simply dispense with these high-sounding rationales, not least because a great many people still credit them, indeed cling to them ever more tenaciously as they feel the ground shifting beneath their feet. The commodity, *pace* Adorno, cannot be its own ideology, at least not yet. One could imagine a future phase of the system of which this would be true, in which it had taken a course at some North American university, desperately or cheerfully jettisoned its own foundations and left behind it the whole business of rhetorical legitimation. Indeed there are those who claim that this is precisely what is afoot today: that 'hegemony' is no longer important, that the system does not care whether we believe in it or not, that it has no need to secure our spiritual complicity as long as we do more or less what it demands. It no longer has to pass through human consciousness to reproduce itself, just to keep that consciousness permanently distracted and rely for its reproduction on its own automated mechanisms. But postmodernism belongs in this respect to a transitional era, one in which the metaphysical, like some unquiet ghost, can neither resuscitate itself nor decently die. If it could manage to lapse from being, then no doubt postmodernism would pass away with it.

I must end, regretfully, on a minatory note. Postmodern end-of-history thinking does not envisage a future for us much different from the present, a prospect it oddly views as a cause for celebration. But there is indeed one such possible future among several, and its name is fascism. The greatest test of postmodernism, or for that matter of any other political doctrine, is how it would shape up to that. Its rich body of work on racism and ethnicity, on the paranoia of identity-thinking, on the perils of totality and the fear of otherness: all this, along with its deepened insights into the cunning of power, would no doubt be of considerable value. But its cultural relativism and moral conventionalism, its scepticism, pragmatism and localism, its distaste for ideas of solidarity and disciplined organization, its lack of any adequate theory of political agency: all these would tell heavily against it. In confronting its political antagonists, the left, now more than ever, has need of strong ethical and even anthropological foundations; nothing short of this is likely to furnish us with the political resources we require. And on this score, postmodernism is in the end part of the problem rather than of the solution.

Notes

1 Beginnings

1 David Morley and Kuan-Hsing Chen (eds), *Stuart Hall: Critical Dialogues* (London, 1996), p. 226.

2 Ambivalences

1 I say postmodernism has *helped* to place these issues on the political agenda; but the women's and civil rights movements actually preceded it, and not all such activists would define their politics in postmodern terms.

2 Peter Osborne, *The Politics of Time* (London, 1995), p. 157.

3 A related postmodern fantasy, once more merely inverting traditional metaphysics, is to claim that the concept of ideology is useless because it implies, as its opposite, some absolute truth. You do not need privileged access to absolute truth to criticize racist discourse.

4 Williams discusses 'an assumption about rationality, to the effect that two considerations cannot be rationally weighed against each other unless there is a common consideration in terms of which they can be compared. This assumption is at once very powerful and utterly baseless. Quite apart from the ethical, aesthetic considerations can be weighed against economic ones (for instance) without being an application of them, and without their both being an example of a third kind of consideration' (*Ethics and the Limits of Philosophy*, Cambridge, Mass., 1985, p. 17).

3 Histories

1 Francis Mulhern (ed.), *Contemporary Marxist Literary Criticism* (London, 1992), p. 22.
2 Theodor W. Adorno, *Negative Dialectics* (London, 1973), p. 320.
3 'Instead of singing the idea of the advent of liberal democracy and the capitalist market in the euphoria of the end of history, instead of celebrating the "end of ideologies" and the end of the great emancipatory discourses, let us never neglect this obvious macroscopic fact, made up of innumerable singular sites of suffering: no degree of progress allows one to ignore that never before, in absolute terms, never have so many men, women and children been subjugated, starved or exterminated on the earth' (Jacques Derrida, *Specters of Marx*, London, 1994, p. 85). One should add, however, that if suffering has indeed increased, so by and large has our sensitivity to it. The importance placed by the modern age on the relief or avoidance of suffering is one mark of its difference from much in pre-Enlightenment societies.
4 Michael Foucault famously views power as enabling; but this is not the same as a moral judgement that it can be beneficial.
5 Such culturalism has also marked so-called post-colonial discourse, which has had much of great value to say of identity, representation and the like, but has often enough evaded questions of economic exploitation. Whatever is centrally at stake between North and South, it is certainly not 'culture'.
6 For a discussion of these and related matters, see my *Ideology: An Introduction* (London, 1991).
7 Ellen Meiksins Wood, 'Introduction', *Monthly Review* (July/Aug. 1995), p. 4.

4 Subjects

1 See Charles Taylor, 'Atomism', in *Philosophy and the Human Sciences: Philosophical Papers, vol. 2* (Cambridge, 1985), pp. 188–210.
2 See R. G. Peffer, *Marxism, Morality, and Social Justice* (Princeton, 1990), Part 1.
3 See for example Alasdair MacIntyre, *After Virtue: A Study in*

Moral Theory (London, 1981) and Charles Taylor, *Sources of the Self* (Cambridge, 1989). For a lucid account of the quarrel between liberals and communitarians from the former standpoint, see Will Kymlicka, *Liberalism, Community and Culture* (Oxford, 1989), ch. 3.

4 This is not some ethnocentric prejudice that only the well-off West can go socialist, just the traditional Marxist insistence that if you try to construct socialism isolated, unaided and in desperately backward conditions, then you are in grave danger of Stalinism. The socialist project can of course be launched where it is currently most urgent, in the exploited neo-colonial territories – but not without aid and solidarity from those nations which have traditionally exploited them, which would then require a socialist transformation of those countries too. This is surely the essential meaning of the claim that socialism must finally be international or nothing.

5 Raymond Williams, *Culture and Society 1780–1950* (Harmondsworth, 1985), pp. 304, 318, 320.

6 For the relations between republican humanism and socialism, see Terry Eagleton, 'Deconstruction and Human Rights', in Barbara Johnson (ed.), *Freedom and Interpretation* (New York, 1993).

7 I have adopted this point from Kymlicka, *Liberalism, Community and Culture*, p. 66.

5 Fallacies

1 Charles Taylor, *Sources of the Self* (Cambridge, 1989), p. 28.

2 Garth L. Hallet, *Essentialism: A Wittgensteinian Critique* (New York, 1991), p. 2. It is, on the whole, a similar kind of strong essentialism which is usefully criticized by Penelope Mackie in 'How Things Might Have Been: A Study in Essentialism' (D.Phil. thesis, University of Oxford, 1987). See also Martha Nussbaum, 'Human Functioning and Social Justice: In Defence of Aristotelian Essentialism', *Political Theory*, 20, no. 2 (1992).

3 See S. Meikle, *Essentialism in the Work of Karl Marx* (London, 1985), and Norman Geras, *Marx and Human Nature* (London, 1983).

4 Denys Turner, *Marxism and Christianity* (Oxford, 1983), p. 86.

5 That this is not in fact necessarily a linear or stagist theory of history was made clear in footnote 4, p. 83, above.

6 See however Horace L. Fairlamb, *Critical Conditions: Postmodernity and the Question of Foundations* (Cambridge, 1994), which argues interestingly for a pluralistic case about epistemological foundations.

7 'Tends to' anti-universalism, since there are postmodern philosophers who do not discard the idea entirely but seek to rework it. I am speaking here rather of the general tenor of postmodern culture, especially in its less astute, more 'popular' forms of thought.

8 Richard Rorty, *Contingency, Irony, and Solidarity* (Cambridge, 1989), p. 191.

9 See Manfred Frank, *What Is Neostructuralism?* (Minneapolis, 1989).

10 A time-warping which demands deeper exploration. The colonial processes which helped, for both good and ill, to deprive third-world societies of a developed modernity have now largely yielded to the neo-colonial processes whereby those still partly pre-modern formations are sucked into the vortex of the West's postmodernity. Postmodernity without an evolved modernity to be consequent to is thus increasingly their destiny, as belatedness gives birth to a form of prematurity. An added contradiction is that this painful tension between the archaic and the avant-garde then, at the cultural level, reproduces something of the classic conditions of a *modernist* art.

11 Taylor, *Sources of the Self*, pp. 67–8.

12 Barbara Hernstein Smith, *Contingencies of Value* (Cambridge, Mass., 1988), p. 94.

13 One should remember that the Unites States is a country with a revolutionary heritage and a fairly recent history of fierce, courageous class struggle, which in 1968 assembled the greatest peace rally history has ever witnessed, one directed against its own government. Those of its radicals who strive to maintain such precious traditions in unpropitious conditions deserve the highest praise.

14 For some postmodern theorists, the term 'plurality' has too singular a ring to it. They thus prefer 'pluralities'. But this may also sound a little restrictive. Perhaps a 'pluralism of pluralities' would be rather less monolithic.

15 Justin Rosenberg, 'Hobsbawm's Century', *Monthly Review*, 47, no. 3 (July/Aug. 1995), p. 154.

Index

Index